ONE WHO YAWNS

Belying his ferocity, courage, determination
and leadership skills, Geronimo's Apache name
translates to One Who Yawns.

**A MODERN HISTORIAN, SUMMING UP
GERONIMO'S TRAITS, SAID,
". . . EITHER YOU LOVE HIM OR YOU HATE HIM."**

Even in his own time, Geronimo drew
contrasting reactions. Read these stories of an
American legend, and you'll start
to understand this fierce warrior, the times
in which he lived, and why extremes marked
the way people saw him.

THESE STORIES
TELL YOU ABOUT GERONIMO

THE FAMILY MAN
THE WARRIOR
THE PRISONER OF WAR

Each of the books in the
WILD WEST COLLECTION
brings you stories of when the Old West was young
and rowdy. They are available in book stores
or from *Arizona Highways* via its Web site
(www.arizonahighways.com), its toll-free telephone
number or mail order. Turn to the back of
this book to learn more about them.

DAYS OF DESTINY
MANHUNTS & MASSACRES
THEY LEFT THEIR MARK
THE LAW OF THE GUN
TOMBSTONE CHRONICLES
STALWART WOMEN
INTO THE UNKNOWN
RATTLESNAKE BLUES
BUCKSKINS, BEDBUGS & BACON
DOUBLE CROSS

Design: MARY WINKELMAN VELGOS
Production: BETH ANDERSON
Front cover photo: NATIONAL ARCHIVES
Tooled leather design on covers: KEVIN KIBSEY AND RONDA JOHNSON
Map: BETH ANDERSON
Copy editors: EVELYN HOWELL AND PK PERKIN McMAHON
Book editor: BOB ALBANO

Published by the Book Division of *Arizona Highways*® magazine, a monthly
publication of the Arizona Department of Transportation, 2039 West Lewis
Avenue, Phoenix, Arizona 85009. Telephone: (602) 712-2200
Web site: www.arizonahighways.com

Publisher — Win Holden
Managing Editor — Bob Albano
Associate Editors — Evelyn Howell and PK Perkin McMahon
Art Director — Mary Winkelman Velgos
Production Director — Cindy Mackey

Printed in the United States
Library of Congress Catalog Number 2002104112
ISBN 1-893860-83-3

GERONIMO!

Stories of an American Legend

by SHARON S. MAGEE

ACKNOWLEDGMENTS

GERONIMO HOLDING A BOW AT MOUNT VERNON, ALABAMA. HE OFTEN SOLD SUCH BOWS AS SOUVENIRS.

As WITH ANY BOOK, MANY PEOPLE HAVE HELPED WITH THIS one, some knowingly, some not. Thanks go to those who were there — Lt. Britton Davis, Charles F. Lummis, Capt. John G. Bourke, John P. Clum, and many others, and those Apaches who shared their stories, Asa Daklugie, Jason Betzinez, James Kaywaykla, Eugene Chihuahua, and especially the old warrior himself, Geronimo — for leaving such a wealth of first-hand information. Thanks also to Angie Debo, Eve Ball, Odie B. Faulk, Frank C. Lockwood, Dan Thrapp, Edwin Sweeney, and Louis Kraft who have interpreted so well this rich mother lode of information.

Also thanks to Alexander Books for permission to quote freely from *Geronimo's Story of His Life*, edited by S.M. Barrett.

A special thanks to the librarians at the Arizona Historical Society in Tucson and the Arizona Room at the Phoenix Central Library, and particularly to Edwin Sweeney, author of *Cochise and Mangas Coloradas*, for his guiding hand, which always keeps me on the straight and narrow.

S HARON S. MAGEE'S FASCINATION with the American Indian and the West began when she was around 9 years old and her parents gave her a membership to a children's history book club. She devoured books on Daniel Boone, Davey Crockett, Cochise, Geronimo, and many others.

This love never left her, although it remained buried during those years when she was earning a living and raising a family. Family grown, she and her husband moved to Arizona in 1988 due to a job transfer. After Sharon took an Arizona history class taught by Marshall Trimble, her interest resurfaced. In that class, she heard a story about a white woman raised as an Apache and the seed of a novel was planted. In doing research on the Apache Wars era for the novel, she found herself riveted by the violent and beautiful history of Arizona and the Apache people.

Although history remains her passion, Sharon has written many articles on an eclectic range of topics for such magazines as *Arizona Highways*, *Priorities*, *The Valley Guide Quarterly*, and *Phoenix Downtown Magazine*.

Sharon has won recognition and awards for her fiction and nonfiction work, including the 2000 Arizona Newspapers Association Award for Outstanding Writing. She and her husband, Stuart Vaughan, live in Phoenix. Between them, they have four children and four grandsons.

Dedicated to the men and women of all races who shaped Arizona's destiny.

CONTENTS

GERONIMO RELAXES UNDER A BRUSH-COVERED RAMADA
IN EXILE AT FORT SILL, INDIAN TERRITORY, OKLAHOMA.

Alope: Geronimo's first love and first of his nine wives. Member of the Nedhni band of the Chiricahua Apaches.

Betzinez, Jason: Geronimo's cousin and member of the Warm Springs band. Wrote *I Rode With Geronimo*.

Chihuahua: Chief of the Warm Springs band.

Chihuahua, Eugene: Son of Warm Springs Chief Chihuahua.

Clum, John: Agent of San Carlos and Fort Apache reservations; later Tombstone mayor. Only man to ever capture Geronimo.

Crook, Gen. George: Instrumental in ending the Apache Wars. Negotiated Geronimo's surrender at Cañon de los Embudos.

Daklugie, Asa: Son of Geronimo's sister, Ishton, and Juh.

Davis, Britton: Army officer and agent at the San Carlos Reservation. Wrote *The Truth About Geronimo*.

Fun: Said "Fun." Geronimo's "brother," probably his cousin. One of Geronimo's best warriors.

Gatewood, Lt. Charles B.: Instrumental in getting Geronimo to agree to surrender to Gen. Nelson A. Miles.

Ih-tedda: Mescalero Apache and one of Geronimo's wives. Their children, Lenna and Robert, were his only ones to survive and continue his line.

Juh: Said "Ho" or "Who." Married Geronimo's favorite sister, Ishton; chief of the Nedhni band.

Kaywaykla, James: Apache youth who went into captivity with Geronimo in 1886. Narrated *In the Days of Victorio*.

Lawton, Capt. Henry A.: Tracked Geronimo in Mexico.

Loco: Chief of the Warm Springs band.

Lozen: Victorio's sister, medicine woman and warrior; often served as Geronimo's courier. Of the Warm Springs band.

Miles, Gen. Nelson A.: Accepted Geronimo's final surrender.

Naiche: Cochise's youngest son. After his brother Taza died, became last chief of the free Chiricahua Apaches.

Nana: Chief of the Warm Springs band. Brother-in-law to Geronimo. Sometimes called Old Nana.

Perico: Geronimo's "brother," probably a cousin; one of his most trusted warriors.

Sieber, Al: Army Chief of Scouts during the Apache Wars.

Victorio: Chief of the Warm Springs band. Died in Mexico.

Wratten, George: White interpreter for the Apaches.

BANDS OF THE CHIRICAHUA APACHE TRIBE

(Toward the end of the Apache Wars, all were simply called Chiricahuas.)

Bedonkohe: Geronimo's band. Around 1860 assimilated by Chiricahua band. Lived in the vicinity of the Gila River and Mogollon Mountains in western New Mexico.

Chiricahua: Also called the Chokonens, led by Cochise. Lived in southeast Arizona in the Chiricahua, Dragoon and Dos Cabezas mountains. Cochise's son Naiche was their last chief.

Nednhi: Meaning the Enemy People, ranged in Mexico's Sierra Madre. Apaches considered them the wildest Chiricahua band. Juh was their best-known chief.

Warm Springs: Also called the Mimbres or Chihennes, the Red Paint People. Lived in the western part of New Mexico. Chiefs included Mangas Coloradas, Victorio, Nana, and Loco.

1823: Goyahkla born, probably in New Mexico.

March 1851: Mexican soldiers massacre Apaches at Janos, Mexico; Goyahkla's wife, children, and mother killed.

Summer 1852: Revenge raid at Arispe; Goyahkla receives name of "Geronimo."

June 1876: Geronimo tricks John Clum and runs to Mexico.

April 21, 1877: John Clum captures Geronimo.

April 4, 1878: Geronimo jumps the San Carlos Reservation and goes to Mexico.

Sept. 30, 1881: Along with Juh and Naiche, Geronimo leaves the San Carlos Reservation for Mexico after Cibecue Massacre.

Mid-April 1882: Stevens Ranch massacre.

April 19, 1882: Geronimo "rescues" Loco and his band from the San Carlos Reservation.

February – March 1884: Returns to San Carlos with cattle.

May 17, 1885: Along with Naiche, Mangus (son of Chief Mangas Coloradas), and Chihuahua, Geronimo jumps the Fort Apache Reservation.

March 27, 1886: Geronimo surrenders to Gen. George Crook at Cañon de los Embudos in Mexico.

March 29-30, 1886: Geronimo flees with 37 of his people back to Sierra Madre in Mexico.

Sept. 4, 1886: Geronimo surrenders to Gen. Nelson A. Miles at Skeleton Canyon in Arizona's Peloncillo Mountains.

Sept. 8, 1886: Apaches leave Bowie Station for Florida.

Sept. 10, 1886: Brig. Gen. D.S. Stanley ordered to hold Apaches in San Antonio.

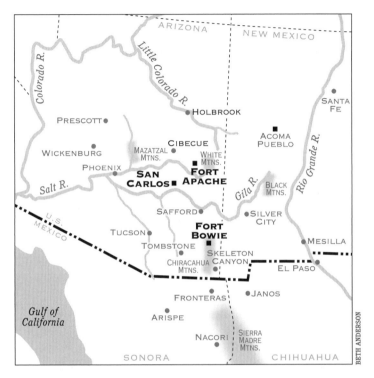

GEOGRAPHICAL SCOPE OF CHAPTERS 1 TO 14

Oct. 22, 1886: Apaches leave San Antonio for Florida.

May 13, 1888: Fort Pickens prisoners transferred to Mount Vernon, Alabama.

Oct. 4, 1894: Apaches exiled to Fort Sill, Oklahoma.

Feb. 17, 1909: Geronimo dies at Fort Sill.

A Life of Transition

*Once called "the wickedest Indian
that ever lived," today the famed Apache warrior
often symbolizes ferocity and bravery.*

———⊰•⊱———

"THE APACHES ARE OUT!"
     These words struck fear into even the stoutest of
hearts living in the Southwest in the late 1800s.
Perhaps no one person has been both hated for the destruction and death he caused and loved for his fierce defense of his homeland than the one most often associated with those words, the Apache war leader, Geronimo. Historian C.L. Sonnichsen said of this "love him or hate him" attitude:

> . . . the two Geronimos have existed side by side almost from the beginning, and they still do exist, but Geronimo the Wicked is barely alive . . . and Geronimo the Good is having things pretty much his own way.

Today, we instantly recognize Geronimo's name and likeness. Books, movies, and television pore over the details of his life, sometimes creating or continuing exaggeration or error about his life. The effect, however, is that his name and image conjure up feelings of ferocity and bravery. World War II paratroopers started a still-practiced tradition by yelling "Geronimo" as they leapt from airplanes. Even today, a paratroop unit calls itself the Geronimo Battalion.

     Transition marked Geronimo's lifetime. Having never seen a white man during his childhood, Geronimo fiercely fought a losing battle for his people's survival and their right to their homeland in the midst of white settlement. He died, not only

**THE FAMILIAR FACE OF
GERONIMO, CHIRICAHUA APACHE**

having adopted the ways of his white adversaries, but also as their prisoner of war.

Once called "the wickedest Indian that ever lived," the true Geronimo falls somewhere between saint and sinner. Tales of his brutality have followed him since he roamed the wilds of the Southwest and Mexico, holding the territory in a clutch of terror. Even his nephew and closest ally in his later years, Asa Daklugie, told writer Eve Ball in *Indeh: An Apache Odyssey*, "Towards the end [before the 1886 surrenders, the U.S.] troops just outnumbered his 500 to 1. So they made Geronimo a monster." He then added, "At times he was."

While Geronimo and his fellow Apaches frequently were cruel, atrocities attributed to them just as frequently were exaggerated, often from the anti-Apache hysteria that swept the Southwest during this time. The difficulty arises in trying to separate fact from legend.

Take the story of Al (Arthur Leslie) and Petra Peck, their baby daughter, and Mrs. Peck's 10-year-old niece, Trini Verdin. When Geronimo and his warriors attacked the Peck ranch, some official accounts said the Indians repeatedly raped Mrs. Peck and cut off her breasts, then swung her baby by the heels, smashing her head against every wall in the little ranch house.

Yet Trini, who saw the attack and was kidnapped by the Apaches, did not report this. The little girl said that an Apache shot her aunt and the baby as Mrs. Peck stepped outside with the baby in her arms.

One erroneous report said Apache beatings left Trini a hunchback for life, and some said the Apaches passed Trini from man to man in the band. Yet J.A. Rivera, a Mexican military officer who interviewed her after her rescue, said, "From her own indications and obvious innocence in the face of questions put to her by her relatives, we deduced that she was not violated at any time, probably out of respect for her tender age." The Mexicans considered Geronimo one of their worst enemies and would in no way whitewash such brutalities.

The Apaches themselves often told different versions of a story. In the story of Francesca, Geronimo's "maybe" 10th wife, he says she was about 17 when Mexicans captured her in 1861. Eugene Chihuahua, who claimed her as his grandmother, told writer Eve Ball that Francesca was "in late middle age" when Mexicans captured her, but in another of his versions to Ball, he said she was captured as a child. Events point to her maybe being captured in 1861, but a tombstone said to be hers at Fort Sill, Oklahoma, dates her life from 1861 to 1901. However, Fort Sill records place her death in 1892. The possibility arises, of course, that the grave said to be hers is merely someone else's.

At President Theodore Roosevelt's inaugural parade, in which Geronimo rode, Daklugie says "we wore only the breech-clouts, belts, moccasins, and our medicine hats." It was January, bitterly cold, and pictures of Geronimo at the parade show him warmly wrapped in a blanket.

The spelling and hyphenation of Apache names also pose

GERONIMO POSING WITH A BOW WHILE AT THE WORLD'S FAIR IN ST. LOUIS, MISSOURI, 1904.

a problem, probably because many people had to spell them phonetically. One such name is that of Cochise's younger son and the last chief of the free Chiricahua Apaches. The common spelling today is "Naiche," but it is spelled in many records as "Natchez(s)," "Nachez," "Nachite," "Nai-chi-ti," "Nachee," or "Na-chise." In this book, you'll notice that some Apache names are hyphenated, while similar ones are not. The Apache language was not a written one in the time of Geronimo, and on the points of spelling and hyphenation, I've trusted particular sources.

Deciphering aging handwritten documents presents another difficulty in spelling. In the case of the principal figure in the Cibecue affair, an Apache also called The Prophet, his name is most often written "Noch-ay-del-klinne." However, Chuck Collins, author of *Apache Nightmare*, states that official records spell the third syllable "det" instead of "del." Because the cross

of the "t" appears very faint, he feels that some historian, possibly Charles Lummis or Dan Thrapp, spelled it with an "l" and
others followed his lead.

You see the problem?

S tories exist of Geronimo's love of children and, conversely,
his brutality to the children of his enemies. (The Apaches
loved their children, but on occasion killed their infants if it
was believed their deaths would help ensure the survival of
the band.) That he killed babies and children is hard to accept,
even knowing that later in life he said, "I wake up groaning
when I remember the helpless little children."

Although often portrayed as a chief, Geronimo was not; he
was a medicine man and war leader. Britton Davis, an Army
officer and Geronimo's adversary, said in his book *The Truth
About Geronimo*, "He had risen to the leadership of a faction of
the warriors by sheer courage, determination, and skill as a
leader." Juh stuttered and Naiche was shy and retiring, so
Geronimo acted as their spokesperson.

Daklugie said, "When Naiche was chief of the Chiricahua,
Geronimo continued to direct the fighting but scrupulously
required the warriors to render to Naiche the respect due a
chief. He acted as leader of war parties, but acted rather in the
relationship of general to commander-in-chief."

I n this book we bring you 19 tales of this larger-than-life person. This is not his biography — we have not covered every
major event in Geronimo's life — but rather a series of vignettes
divided into three segments: The Family Man, The Warrior, and
The Prisoner of War.

GERONIMO!
The Family Man

GERONIMO WITH DAUGHTER EVA, SON FENTON,
PROBABLY HIS GRANDDAUGHTER NINA
DAHKEYA, AND ZI-YEH, ONE OF HIS WIVES,
IN A WATERMELON PATCH AT FORT SILL.

An Idyllic Childhood

His Apache name, Goyahkla, meaning
One Who Yawns, doesn't match the spirited
Geronimo of Southwest history.

———◆———

"I ROLLED ON THE DIRT FLOOR OF MY FATHER'S TEPEE, HUNG
in my *tsoch* [cradleboard] at my mother's back or sus-
pended from the bough of a tree. I was warmed by the
sun, rocked by the winds, and sheltered by the trees as other
Indian babes," Geronimo reminisced in his autobiography,
Geronimo's Story of His Life, narrated through his nephew, Asa
Daklugie, to editor S.M. Barrett.

He said he "was born in No-doyohn Cañon, Arizona, June
1829," although events in his life indicate he was probably born
earlier, nearer 1823.

Debate has raged for years over the location of his birthplace. For a long time, historians believed this spot was near
Clifton, Arizona. Geronimo himself said he was born in Arizona,
but his nephew, Daklugie, said the Gila "has three forks 200 or
so miles northeast" of the Clifton location. "It was on the middle
fork of the Gila that the canyon in which they lived is located."
Historians now locate his birthplace in New Mexico along one
of the Gila River forks.

His parents named him Goyahkla, meaning One Who
Yawns. The sleepy, passive character suggested by this name
doesn't match the spirited Geronimo of Southwest history.

Goyahkla's father, son of the great Apache Chief Mahko,
was named Taklishim, The Gray One, and was a member of
the Bedonkohe band of the Chiricahua Apaches. Goyahkla's
mother — although she was a full-blooded Apache — carried

the Mexican name of Juana or Juanita, indicating she may have been a captive in Mexico at one time.

Apaches coddled their children, and certainly Goyahkla received his share. "With my brothers and sisters I played about my father's home," he said. Later in life, Goyahkla mentioned three brothers and four sisters; in reality, all but one sister, Nah-dos-te, were his cousins; Apaches had no word to distinguish between siblings and cousins.

Apache children had fun playing hide and seek and war games, imitating adult behavior, playing with handmade toys, and hunting berries and nuts. Often the children "would steal away to a place several miles distant, where they played all day free from tasks," he remembered. "They were never punished for these frolics." As with all young children, Goyahkla "wore very little clothing in winter and none in the summer," he said.

Ceremony enriched Apache life. When Goyahkla was 4 days old, his parents hired a medicine man to perform a ceremony blessing his cradleboard. When he took his first steps, his parents held a moccasin ceremony to bless his first moccasins. And when he was somewhat more than a year old, his parents blessed him with a haircutting ceremony.

When children reached the age of understanding, their elders taught them Apache traditions and oral history. Taklishim tutored his son on hunting and warfaring traditions, while Juana instructed him in the legends and myths of the supernaturals and prayers to the Apache god Ussen. Also ingrained into his being were those creatures — both good and evil, including the dreaded ghosts and witches — who controlled the Apaches' daily lives.

When he was about 5, the adults separated him and the other boys from the girls. His training as a useful member of adult society had begun.

He learned how to make and use weapons and tools, care for the horses, and tend the family's crops of corn, beans, and pumpkins that grew on about 2 acres. He undoubtedly helped with the making of *tizwin*, a mild corn liquor.

Goyahkla also trained in the basics of war. Games, which

had been fun, now became serious. Goyahkla competed in arrow shooting, racing, wrestling, and the sacred game of hoop-and-pole, which custom dictated only boys and men could play.

Both boys and girls learned to creep and freeze. While the maneuver seemed like a game, it taught the survival technique of remaining motionless for hours when hiding from an enemy. Physical training was important to young Goyahkla and his peers , boys and girls. Being physically fit could mean the difference between life and death, and being able to run for long distances without tiring was essential. Apaches quickly assessed confrontational situations, and if enemy numbers weighed heavily against them, or if danger threatened the women and children, they usually opted to run, literally. In no way was retreat considered cowardice; survival was the prime guiding force of Apache existence.

The boys' training was brutal. The warriors required them to bathe even when ice skinned a river or lake. Youths ran for long distances, both on flat land and up mountains, while holding water in their mouths to prove they were breathing correctly through their noses. Hitting the bark and trunk of a tree with their bare hands and pulling up saplings by the roots provided them strength training.

Although trained for war as a boy, Goyahkla rembered his early life as being filled with peace. "[W]e had never seen a missionary or a priest. We had never seen a white man. Thus quietly lived the Bedonkohe Apaches," he recalled.

Still, the young Goyahkla and his friends listened, entranced, to stories of the battle exploits of his grandfather Mahko, who died before Goyahkla was born. They dreamed of emulating the old chief's feats.

Most boys joined the men on hunting expeditions by the time they turned 14. Goyahkla, however, apparently was a prodigy.

"When I was about 8 or 10 years old, I began to follow the chase, and to me this was never work," he said.

Herds of deer, antelope, and elk roamed the land. He rode

down rabbits and turkeys with his horse and killed them with a club. In the mountains he hunted cougar with bow and arrow and spear. They provided food and skins, which he made into quivers — "they were very pretty and very durable," he recalled. He also hunted eagles for their feathers. "It required great skill to steal upon an eagle, for besides having sharp eyes, he is wise and never stops at any place where he does not have a good view of the surrounding country."

As Goyahkla entered his teen years, social ceremonies took on new meaning. Since age 5 or 6, boys and girls had little contact with each other. Thus, social occasions, which involved dancing with a partner of the opposite sex, gave them the opportunity for a little supervised courting. "I was always glad when the dances and the feasts were announced," he said. "So were all the other young people."

Before Goyahkla reached his maturity, Taklishim died after a long illness. His family and friends bathed him and dressed him in his best clothes, painted his face red, and wrapped him in his finest blanket. They then placed him on his favorite horse along with all his belongings. With loud wails and dressed in their oldest clothes, Goyahkla, his family, and a few of his father's closest friends took Taklishim into the hills, where they placed him in a cave. With him, they buried all his possessions, including his horse so he would have a ride to the spirit world. They then sealed the cave and told no one of its location, nor did they ever visit it.

After his father's death, Goyahkla became the sole support of his widowed mother and his sisters.

His idyllic childhood had ended.

Alope — His First Love

*"Perhaps the greatest joy to me was that
I could marry the fair Alope," Geronimo said
of his becoming a warrior at 17.*

———※———

A FTER HIS FATHER DIED DURING GOYAHKLA'S TEEN YEARS, he and his mother, Juana, decided a change of scene would ease their grief. They planned a visit to relatives and friends living with the Nednhi Apache in Mexico's Sierra Madre. In approximately 1840, Goyahkla and Juana, along with 10 to 15 members of their band, headed for Mexico. Treacherous and difficult, the trip required that they be alert for Mexicans and search for Nednhi trails to concealed watering holes and camps.

Soon after the weary band arrived in the Sierra Madre stronghold, Goyahkla met and fell in love with a Nednhi girl, Alope, whom he later described as "slender, delicate."

He also renewed a friendship he made years before with a bullying, hulking youth named Juh — pronounced "Who" or "Ho." Geronimo considered Juh "as a brother to me."

The two boys had spent hours hunting and playing war games. Juh developed another interest — the beautiful Ishton, Goyahkla's sister. After he became a Nednhi war leader, Juh married her.

Goyahkla joined Juh and other Nednhi warriors on raids against Mexican villages, ranches, and pack trains. As did all potential warriors, he served first as an apprentice, caring for the horses, preparing food, hauling water and wood, and standing guard. The Council of Warriors required an apprentice to perform courageously on four missions before accepting him as a warrior. Goyahkla obviously qualified.

"Being 17 years of age, I was admitted to the Council of Warriors," he noted. "Then I was very happy, for I could go wherever I wanted and do whatever I liked. I could go on the warpath with my tribe. This would be glorious."

His "greatest joy," however, was that "now I could marry the fair Alope." Although Apache custom dictated restraint in sexual matters, Geronimo said, "We had been lovers for a long time."

Protocol called for a representative of Goyahkla to approach Alope's family and make the marriage and dowry arrangements. But he was never big on protocol. "As soon as the council granted me these [warrior] privileges," he said, "I went to see her father concerning our marriage."

Her father was not too keen on losing his favorite daughter to this upstart warrior from the north.

"Perhaps he wanted to keep Alope with him," Geronimo said, "for she was a dutiful daughter; at any rate he asked many ponies for her. I made no reply, but in a few days appeared before his wigwam with the herd of ponies and took with me Alope. This was all the marriage ceremony necessary in our tribe."

Later, he, Alope, and his mother returned to Arizona and the Bedonkohe band. He settled into a life of contentment:

> Not far from my mother's tepee I had made for us a new home. The tepee was made of buffalo hides and in it were many bear robes, lion [cougar] hides, and other trophies of the chase, as well as my spears, bows, and arrows. Alope had made many decorations of beads and drawn work on buckskin . . . She also drew many pictures on the walls of our home. She was a good wife, but she was never strong. We followed the traditions of our fathers and were happy. Three children came to us — children that played, loitered, and worked as I had done.

By 1850, the Bedonkohe were led by a great Apache chief, Mangas Coloradas, a peaceable man of ample height and bulk.

In Mexico, however, continued Apache raiding devastated the countryside. The state of Chihuahua decided to make peace with the Apaches, hoping to stop their depredations. They invited the Apaches to their villages to trade furs and hides for cloth, beads, knives, and other necessities. On June 24, 1850, the Mexicans and the Apaches confirmed the peace agreement.

In March 1851, Mangas Coloradas led his people into Mexico on a trading expedition with the townspeople of Casas Grandes. At this time, Goyahkla was a young warrior, no more significant than any other. As this was a peaceful mission, Alope, their three children, and Juana came with him.

At Janos, Chihuahua, they stopped to trade and camped some distance away. Each morning the men went into town, while a small group stayed behind to guard the camp, women, and children. Each morning they specified a place to rendezvous if trouble arose.

It did. Col. José Maria Carrasco, commander of the military in Sonora, crossed the border of the two Mexican states with 400 soldiers. In their path lay the Apache party camped near Janos.

One afternoon as Goyahkla and the other men walked back to their camp, some women and children ran up to them, telling them Mexicans had attacked. Many Apaches lay dead or had been captured.

Instantly the surviving Apaches scattered. All would meet at the rendezvous spot — a thicket by the Janos River — after nightfall. Geronimo's words, many decades later, still convey the horror and grief of those next few hours:

> [W]hen all were counted, I found that my aged mother, my young wife, and my three small children were among the slain. There were no lights in camp, so without being noticed I silently turned away and stood by the river. How long I stood there I do not know.

They had only 80 warriors left, no weapons, and were inside Mexican territory. Mangas Coloradas gave the order to start back to Arizona without attacking the Mexicans or recovering the dead.

From Geronimo's account:

> I stood until all had passed, hardly knowing what I would do. I did not pray, nor did I resolve to do anything in particular, for I had no purpose left. I finally followed the tribe silently, keeping just within hearing distance of the soft noise of the feet of the retreating Apaches.

Although Geronimo did not say in his autobiography how he knew his family was dead rather than captured, he apparently slipped away from the stunned and grieving Apaches and returned to the camp. Years later, he told a friend at Fort Sill, Oklahoma, that he had seen their bodies lying in a pool of blood.

For two days and three nights, the Apaches marched silently back to Arizona. Just before crossing the border, they stopped to rest and eat. Here Goyahkla discovered "none had lost as I had, for I had lost all." When he reached home:

> There were the decorations that Alope had made — and there were the playthings of our little ones. I burned them all, even our tepee. I also burned my mother's tepee . . . I had vowed vengeance upon the Mexican troopers who had wronged me, and wherever I saw anything to remind me of former happy days my heart would ache for revenge upon Mexico.

Geronimo neither forgot nor forgave the terrible loss he suffered at Janos. For the rest of his life, he searched for ways to wreak vengeance on the Mexicans. In his later years, he said, "I am old now and shall never go on the warpath again, but if I were young, and followed the warpath, it would lead into Old Mexico."

CHAPTER THREE

Loving Husband and Father

*"As sure as the trees bud and bloom
in the spring, so sure is my hope of seeing
you again," Geronimo wrote to his family.
"I think you have influence
with the sun, moon and stars."*

———

A FIERCE AND CRUEL ADVERSARY, GERONIMO WAS ALSO A
loving husband and father. He had at least nine wives.
He sometimes had as many as three at once, "over-
lapping" them, as his nephew Daklugie put it.

When Geronimo married Chee-hash-kish and then
Nana-tha-thtith shortly after Mexicans killed his first wife, Alope,
he entered his first plural marriage. Angie Debo, in *Geronimo: The
Man, His Time, His Place*, said of his marriage to Nana-tha-thtith,
"This marriage indicates his rising importance in the tribe. Only
a superior hunter and raider could support two wives."

Family considerations influenced many of his major de-
cisions. The death of his first family caused his campaign of
vengeance against the Mexicans, and the promise to reunite
him with his family already in captivity weighed heavily in his
decision to surrender to Gen. Nelson A. Miles in 1886.

Marriage gave Geronimo family status with several of the
major players in the Apache Wars: His fourth wife, She-gha,
was closely related to Cochise; his favorite sister, Ishton, married Juh, chief of the Nednhi Apache; and another sister,
Nah-dos-te, married Nana, chief of the Warm Springs Apaches.

Geronimo even had a white father-in-law, Jelikine or Pine Pitch House, the father of his sixth wife, Zi-yeh.

During the years he roamed the Southwest, Geronimo married seven women. Enemies in Mexico and Arizona Territory either killed or captured four of his wives — Alope, Chee-hash-kish, Nana-tha-thtith, and Shtsha-she. In the last half of the 1880s, with armies from both sides of the border chasing him, only She-gha, Zi-yeh, and Ih-tedda remained with him.

As 1886 dawned, hiding from the U.S. soldiers became impossible for the Apaches. Their inevitable surrender came in September, the major enticement for them being reunion with family members already in captivity in Florida. For Geronimo, this meant Zi-yeh and Ih-tedda; She-gha was with him in Arizona.

Despite promises, the government sent the warriors to Fort Pickens at Pensacola on Florida's west coast and the women, children, and former Army scouts to Fort Marion at St. Augustine on Florida's east coast.

At Fort Marion, She-gha joined Ih-tedda and Zi-yeh; Ih-tedda gave birth to a daughter, Lenna; and Geronimo's sickly daughter and a grandchild (Chappo and Nocton's daughter) died.

Geronimo's loneliness and affection for his family showed in poignant love letters he wrote to them with the help of interpreter George Wratten. The only letter to survive, one he sent to two of his wives (probably Ih-tedda and Zi-yeh) and two children (probably Lenna and Fenton), said in part:

> I am very satisfied here, but if I only had you with me again I would be more so. As sure as the trees bud and bloom in the spring, so sure is my hope of seeing you again. I think of God, the President, and you in the same light. I like you so well. When I get your letter I will think well over it. I hope you think the same of me as I do you. I think you have influence with the sun, moon and stars. Write me soon a lovely letter. Your husband, Geronimo.

In early 1887, after an eight-month separation, the Apache women and children of Geronimo's band joined their husbands

THE APACHES, INCLUDING BABIES IN CRADLEBOARDS, IMPRISONED AT FORT MARION, FLORIDA.

and fathers at Fort Pickens. The rest of the Fort Marion Apaches were relocated to Mount Vernon Barracks in Alabama.

The Pensacolian newspaper said, "We suppose that Geronimo's cup of happiness is overflowing now that he is surrounded by his papooses and wives." And indeed it was. His family was again complete.

Geronimo's tender affection for his wives and children amazed visitors to Fort Pickens. One tourist noted, "Geronimo is a terrible old villain, yet he seemed quiet enough today nursing a baby [Lenna]." A reporter noted, "Naiche and Geronimo are better husbands, although much married, than some hod carriers, and know more of their children than do some of the sporting fraternity."

Geronimo's happiness proved short-lived. She-gha, ill with tuberculosis when transferred from crowded, damp Fort Marion, died in September. He buried her in Barrancas National Cemetery, the only Apache buried there. Today her tombstone rests under the protective boughs of an ancient tree.

The next year, 1888, the Fort Pickens prisoners joined the other Apaches at Mount Vernon. Disease continued to take its toll. When word came that Mescalero Apaches could return to their New Mexico reservation, Geronimo sent the pregnant Ih-tedda, who was a Mescalero, and their daughter, Lenna, home with them. Ih-tedda protested tearfully, for she loved Geronimo.

"We were not healthy in this place," Geronimo explained later, "and I consented to let one of my wives go. This separation is according to our custom equivalent to what the white people call divorce, and so she married again soon after she got to Mescalero. She also kept our two small children, which she had a right to do."

Against her bitter protests, Ih-tedda's parents married her to a Mescalero man two or three days after she reached the reservation. Geronimo's son Robert was born shortly afterward.

Geronimo biographer Angie Debo notes, "The sequel was to vindicate Geronimo's judgment. [Ih-tedda's] children were the only ones who were to live to perpetuate his family."

From that time on, Geronimo said, he "never had more than one wife at a time," possibly acquiescing to the White Eyes' view of morality. In 1889, Zi-yeh bore him his last child, his beloved Eva. A visitor wrote of seeing Geronimo hauling Eva "in a child's little express wagon, and seeming quite proud of his employment."

While still in Alabama, Geronimo suffered another heartbreak. His son Chappo, whom a local paper called an "unusually bright young Indian," returned from the Carlisle Indian School in the last stages of tuberculosis. He died on September 9, 1894, and Geronimo buried him in the Mobile National Cemetery. Geronimo, along with Zi-yeh and Chappo's sister, Dohn-say, attended the funeral.

At Fort Sill, Geronimo and Zi-yeh set up housekeeping, trying hard to be "white." After being invited to dinner by the couple, a visitor said Zi-yeh served a "good, clean meal" that they ate with their fingers from a board placed between them on the ground. Two years later, he visited again and this time ate an excellent meal, including dessert, at a "well-set, linen-covered table."

As the new century neared, Zi-yeh's health failed, and Geronimo did all the housework, keeping their home immacu-

IN MEXICO, 1886, FROM RIGHT: GERONIMO WITH HIS BROTHER, FUN; HIS SON, CHAPPO; AND YANOZHA.

late. By now he had lost his son, Fenton, and his daughter, Dohn-say, and her husband and children, except Thomas Dahkeya, who was away at boarding school. (Thomas would die when just 18 years old.)

Zi-yeh died in 1904. On Christmas Day, 1905, Geronimo married his eighth wife, a mystery woman named Sousche or Mrs. Mary Loto, an Apache widow with a grown son. This may have been the woman called Marianetta, sometimes named as one of his wives.

Of this marriage, Geronimo said only, "I married another woman but we could not live happily and separated. She went home to her people—that is an Apache divorce."

Eva, then 16 years old, became his life; he adored her. "Nobody could be kinder to a child than he was to her," an observer noted.

Geronimo gave her an elaborate puberty ceremony but forbade her from marrying. He feared she would not survive childbirth because of her petiteness. She did marry after Geronimo's death and bore a daughter who died at age 2 months. Eva died a year later of tuberculosis.

In 1907 Geronimo married his ninth and final wife,

GERONIMO'S WIVES AND CHILDREN

Alope: At age 17, Geronimo married "the fair Alope," his first and greatest love. They had three children. In 1851 Mexican troops killed Alope, their children, and his mother.

Chee-hash-kish: Around 1852, while still grieving for Alope, he married Chee-hash-kish. The marriage lasted 30 years until Mexicans captured her in 1882. Their son, Chappo, and daughter, Dohn-say, joined Geronimo in his final struggle for freedom, and ultimate surrender and imprisonment. Dohn-say had three children, all of whom died young. Chappo had one daughter, born to his wife, Nocton, during the march into Fort Bowie after Geronimo's surrender to Gen. Nelson A. Miles in 1886. The infant died soon after reaching Fort Marion in Florida and Nocton died after their transfer to Alabama.

Nana-tha-thtith: She became the third Mrs. Geronimo shortly after he married Chee-hash-kish; they had one child. Mexicans killed Nana-tha-thtith and the child.

She-gha: Sometime in the late 1860s or early 1870s, Geronimo married She-gha, a relative of Cochise. She rode with him until his surrender in 1886 and went into captivity with him.

Shtsha-she: Around 1878, Geronimo married Shtsha-she, about whom little is known. It is believed she died at Fort Apache after being captured by U.S. soldiers.

Zi-yeh: In 1882, a "diminutive Nednhi girl named Zi-yeh," whose white father was "an Apache in all but blood" caught Geronimo's fancy and soon became his sixth wife. She bore him Fenton and his precious Eva.

Ih-tedda: In 1885, Geronimo and his warriors captured a party of Mescalero women and children, including Ih-tedda (Young Girl). After offering her to his chief, Naiche, and finding him "well supplied," Geronimo took Ih-tedda as his seventh wife. She bore the only two children to give Geronimo descendents, Lenna and Robert.

Mary Loto: On Christmas Day, 1905, Geronimo married a mystery woman named Sousche or Mrs. Mary Loto. The marriage ended in divorce.

Azul: In 1907 Geronimo married Sunsetso (Old Lady Yellow) or Azul, who nursed him through his final illness in 1909. Azul never remarried.

**GERONIMO'S NIECE, EMILY,
AND HIS LAST CHILD, EVA.**

Sunsetso (Old Lady Yellow in Apache) or Azul (Blue in Spanish); it's not clear why she had names of two different colors. She nursed him through his final illness in 1909. Azul never remarried. When the government released the Apaches from prisoner-of-war status in 1913, she moved to the Mescalero Reservation in New Mexico. During World War I, Mrs. Geronimo, as everyone called her, bought a war bond and wore a Red Cross button.

Geronimo lives on through his children by Ih-tedda. Robert, who died in 1966, had four children, and was considered the most successful stockman on the Mescalero Reservation; he served as president of the Cattlegrowers Association there. Lenna, who died in 1918, also left descendants.

CHAPTER FOUR

Did Geronimo Marry the Brave Francesca?

She escaped Mexican slavery only to have to fight off an attacking mountain lion.

G ERONIMO HAD AT LEAST NINE WIVES, AND VAGUE HINTS indicate maybe more. Francesca, for instance. Eugene Chihuahua claimed her as his maternal grandmother and told Francesca's story to Eve Ball, who recorded it in *Indeh: An Apache Odyssey*: Mexicans captured her and three younger women, so the story goes, to sell as slaves in Mexico. A maguey, or agave, farmer from Mexico City bought them. He named the older woman Francesca and made her his housekeeper and put the three younger women to work in the maguey fields.

They slaved for the Mexican farmer for five years, all the time plotting escape. Knowing they needed a weapon, Francesca stole a butcher knife and hid it in a scabbard attached to her belt under her long skirt, within easy reach.

The farmer sometimes let the women attend a small church outside the city's north gate, so Francesca picked an evening when many people would be attending services. The four women's peon dress ensured they fit in with the other worshipers. Instead of entering the church, they walked on into the dark, carrying just their blankets and the stolen knife. They hid by day and walked by night, eating prickly pear cactus fruit.

After many nights, they knew by the terrain that they were close to Arizona and felt safe enough to rest. They stopped by a tree-shaded stream and built a brush tepee. The night air carried a chill, and the women wrapped up in their blankets.

Francesca pulled hers close around her neck. As they lay in their leafy tepee, a mountain lion crashed in. It grabbed Francesca by the throat, clawing at her face and tearing her scalp. Then, it dragged her from the tepee by her shoulder. The other women hit the lion with clubs and rocks while Francesca struggled to reach her knife. Grasping it, she stabbed the lion repeatedly until she struck its heart, killing it.

The lion had gravely injured Francesca, although the blanket had protected her throat from a mortal wound. Her scalp hung by a strip of skin, so the women bound it in place with buckskin thongs. Not having any herbs or medicine, they relied on an old remedy and rubbed the dead lion's saliva on her open wounds. At daybreak, they picked cactus pads, burnt off the thorns, slit them open, and placed the open sides against the wounds. In three or four weeks, Francesca felt fit to travel, and they finally reached Warm Springs in New Mexico.

Years later, at Fort Sill, Oklahoma, Francesca remained unmarried; her disfigured face had discouraged suitors. (Evidently, she gave birth to Eugene Chihuahua's mother at some time before being taken by the Mexicans.) "Geronimo said that she deserved a good husband because she was the bravest of all Apache women," Chihuahua said. "So he married her. He had plenty of wives, anyway."

Did Geronimo marry this brave woman? His own words belie the probability. After his wife She-gha died in 1887, he said, "I never had more than one wife at a time." At that time he was also married to Zi-yeh and stayed married to her until her death in 1904. Then he married Mary Loto and, after divorcing her, Azul.

While the story of Francesca and the lion is legend among the Apaches, only Chihuahua's story mentions marriage to Geronimo. Geronimo tells her story in his memoirs, but calls her "Francisco." He clearly admired her, but hints at nothing else.

GERONIMO!

The Warrior

**GERONIMO IN MEXICO,
AS PHOTOGRAPHED BY
C.S. FLY IN 1886.**

The Renaming of Goyahkla

When the young warrior Goyahkla led a revenge battle against the Mexicans, he was to make a name for himself that is remembered to this day.

———◆———

I**N MARCH 1851, MEXICAN SOLDIERS ATTACKED PART OF AN** Apache trading party and killed Geronimo's wife, his children, and his mother, a loss so devastating it forever colored his life. He vowed vengeance upon the Mexican troopers.

Chief Mangas Coloradas also plotted revenge and sent Geronimo, still known as Goyahkla, the one most affected by the massacre, to recruit other bands within the Chiricahua tribe.

Goyahkla first approached Cochise and the Chokenen Apaches in the Chiricahua Mountains of southeastern Arizona. He later said Cochise called a council at dawn, then signalled him to rise and present his cause to the gathered warriors.

Exhorting them to follow him, Goyahkla said, "I will fight in the front of the battle. If I am killed, no one need mourn for me. My people have all been killed in that country, and I, too, will die if need be."

Cochise's warriors voted to go on the warpath.

Goyahkla then approached Juh of the Nednhi, his brother-in-law and good friend and ally, who lived in Mexico's Sierra Madre. Juh "immediately issued orders for a council," Geronimo recalled, and the Nednhi promised to help.

T**he next summer — one year after the massacre — they** gathered at the Mexican border. Geronimo recalled:

Their faces were painted, the war bands fastened upon their brows, their long scalp locks ready for the hand and knife of the warrior who could overcome them. None of us were mounted and each warrior wore moccasins and also a cloth wrapped about his loins. Each warrior carried three days' rations.

They also carried fire drills and pollen to bring them victory. The war party set out in three columns led by Mangas Coloradas, Cochise, and Juh. Geronimo remembered, "We usually marched about 14 hours per day, making three stops for meals, and traveling 40 to 45 miles a day."

Traveling along riverbeds and through the mountains via routes known only to the Apaches, they reached Arispe, Sonora, where the soldiers who had attacked Goyahkla's family at Janos, Chihuahua, were billeted. It occupied high ground along the western bank of the Sonora River.

With the mountains behind them, a few of the Apaches showed themselves to the citizens of the town, setting off a frenzy. A peace delegation of eight men with jingling spurs rode out from Arispe to parley with the Apaches. "These we captured, killed, and scalped. This was to draw the troops from the city, and the next day they came," Geronimo said.

They skirmished all day without a major engagement. As evening came, the Apaches captured the Mexicans' supply train, providing them well with food and additional weapons.

The next day, the entire Mexican force, two companies of cavalry and two of infantry, joined the attack. For the first time, Goyahkla led a battle: "[The chieftans] said I might direct the battle. Because I had been more deeply wronged than others, this honor was conferred upon me."

In his element, Goyahkla led the attack. He formed the Apaches into a crescent in the timber near the river. As the Mexicans advanced, the Apaches began to close the crescent. Soon they had the Mexicans surrounded.

"In all the battle I thought of my murdered mother, wife,

and babies, of my father's grave, and my vow of vengeance, and I fought with fury," Geronimo recalled. "Many fell by my hand, and constantly I led the advance."

Time and again, he charged from the woods and attacked the Mexican soldiers with his spear, taking their rifles back to the woods to give to Cochise, for he did not know how to use a rifle. He had no fear for his own life; his Power had told him after his family's death that no bullet would ever kill him.

Soon, a cry of fear went up from the Mexican soldiers. "*Cuidado!* [Watch out!] *Geronimo!*" Then the Apaches took up the chant, and the Apache named Goyahkla became the man and warrior known as Geronimo.

After two hours, only Geronimo and three other Apaches remained on the battlefield; their fellow warriors had pulled back into the woods and mountains. Two Mexican soldiers rode out and shot two of the men; the third warrior fell to a Mexican saber as he and Geronimo turned and ran toward safety.

Geronimo grabbed a spear and turned to face the two horsemen. One fell with a well-placed thrust. Grabbing that horseman's saber, Geronimo grappled with the other soldier on the ground. Geronimo discarded the saber and, using his knife, killed his enemy.

"Over the bloody field covered with the bodies of Mexicans, rang the fierce Apache war-whoop," Geronimo recalled. "I could not call back my loved ones, I could not bring back the dead Apaches, but I could rejoice in this revenge."

Why did the Mexicans cry "Geronimo"? It is most often thought they were calling on St. Jerome — Geronimo in Spanish — to save them from the devil Apache they would come to know all too well.

A Broken Promise
or a Scheme to Survive?

*Geronimo's sense of honor and truth
often clashed with the white man's when it came
to ensuring his people's survival. John P. Clum,
agent on the San Carlos Reservation,
learned this point the hard way.*

———◆———

IN 1876, THE CHIRICAHUA APACHES LIVED ON A RESERVATION in the Chiricahua Mountains of southeastern Arizona Territory, supervised by agent Tom Jeffords.

Geronimo remembered the time as peaceful. The United States government, however, still received complaints about the Apaches from Mexican officials. Located close to the border, the Apaches often left the reservation to raid Mexican villages and ranches. The U.S. government sought an excuse to close the reservation and move the Chiricahuas north to San Carlos. A disagreement among Apaches, leaving several Apaches dead, gave Federal officials their excuse.

Geronimo explained, "Some Indians at the post were drunk on *tizwin*, which they had made from corn. They fought among themselves and four of them were killed."

The truth was more complicated. When Cochise died in June 1874, the Chiricahuas named his eldest son, Taza, as his successor. Two of Taza's most vocal opponents were Skinya, a contender for the chieftainship (chiefs were elected, so being a chief's son was a plus, but not a guarantee), and Skinya's brother Pionsenay. When the disagreement became too heated,

TAZA, COCHISE'S SON AND CHIRICAHUA CHIEF

Skinya, Pionsenay, and their small band left the main band, moving to the Dragoon Mountains about 40 miles west of the Chiricahua Mountains.

Against Jeffords' orders, Nick Rodgers, the station keeper at Sulphur Springs, sold whiskey to these disgruntled Apaches, but then refused to sell them more. Drunk and angry, Skinya's Apaches killed Rodgers and two other white men.

The killings sent Arizona Territory into an uproar. The *Arizona Citizen* in Tucson advocated the "slaying of Chiricahua men, women, and children until every valley and crest and crag, and fastness shall send to high heaven the grateful incense of festering and rotting Chiricahuas."

J.Q. Smith, Commissioner of Indian Affairs, sent a telegram to John P. Clum, the agent at the San Carlos Reservation:

Proceed to Chiricahua; take charge of Indians and agency property there, suspending Agent Jeffords, for which this dispatch shall be your full authority. If practicable, remove Chiricahua Indians to San Carlos.

While normally at odds with the military, in this instance Clum insisted on being "properly supported." In addition to the 54 Apache police he took with him, 550 soldiers of the 6th Cavalry and 100 Apache scouts under Brevet Maj. Gen. August V. Kautz made post haste for the reservation, backing up Clum during the removal of the Chiricahuas.

Clum reached Sulphur Springs on the afternoon of June 4, 1876. That same night, Skinya, Pionsenay, and their warriors visited Taza and his younger brother, Naiche, lobbying Taza's band to join them. A fight broke out. Naiche killed Skinya, while Taza wounded Pionsenay. Six others were killed as well.

Around noon the next day, Clum and his police force arrived at the Chiricahua agency where Taza and Naiche greeted them.

"I explained to them fully the purpose of my visit, and they readily consented to the removal of their band to the San Carlos Reservation," Clum reported.

Jeffords told Clum that Geronimo, Juh, and another leader named Nolgee, also living on the Chiricahua reservation, wanted to meet with him. Clum later noted, "I had never before heard of Geronimo. I sent for the chiefs, and we had a big smoke and a big talk on June 8."

Geronimo told Clum that he and his people were willing to go to San Carlos. However, he said, his people were about 20 miles away, and he needed time to round them up.

"The general demeanor of this renegade did not inspire complete confidence," Clum said. "Accordingly, I ordered some of my scouts to shadow his movements."

After negotiating a four-day pass, Geronimo, Juh, and Nolgee raced back to their camp. Their people packed, discarding all except essential belongings. They killed their dogs to keep them from barking. They also killed feeble and disabled

CHIEF VICTORIO WAS KILLED IN MEXICO IN 1880.

horses, which would slow the band's movement, and white horses, which would be visible at night. By the time the scouts raced back and told Clum of the Apaches' defection, and he informed the military, Geronimo and his people were miles away.

This was the first of Geronimo's several breakouts. He felt his actions ensured his people's survival. Clum, however, considered the escape an unpardonable breech of trust.

"I do not think that I ever belonged to those soldiers at Apache Pass, or that I should have asked them where I might go," Geronimo later said. "We deemed it impossible to keep the different bands together in peace. Therefore, we separated, each leader taking his own band. Some of them went to San Carlos and some to Old Mexico, but I took my tribe back to Hot [Warm] Springs and rejoined Victorio's band," in New Mexico."

Many years later, Geronimo's nephew Asa Daklugie said, "What right had this arrogant young man [Clum] to tell them what to do?"

Authority on the Warm Springs reservation was lax, allowing Geronimo and others to stage raids into Mexico. John M.

Shaw, the Warm Springs agent, reported him there on July 21, along with 40 Chiricahua Apaches and one of his wives. His presence angered many of the Warm Springs Apaches.

"We were on friendly terms with the towns around us and we were causing no trouble there," groused one to ethnologist Morris Opler years later. "But the Chiricahuas and the Nednhi came around. They used to bring in horses stolen from the south and they got us into trouble."

When the Apaches complained about Geronimo to their chief, Victorio, he remarked, "These people are not bothering us."

He was to find out just how much bother they really were.

In March 1877, Geronimo, along with six other Apache leaders and a group of their followers, appeared on the Warm Springs reservation with 100 head of horses and cattle. Geronimo demanded the rations he had missed while raiding in Mexico. When the agent refused, Geronimo became irate. Commissioner Smith responded with a directive to Clum:

> If practicable, take your Indian police and arrest renegade Indians at Ojo Caliente [Warm Springs], New Mexico. Seize stolen horses in their possession; restore property to rightful owners. Remove renegades to San Carlos and hold them in confinement for murder and robbery. Call on military for aid, if needed.

Clum, who hated Geronimo for tricking him the year before, began the 400-mile trip on foot. He later called this mission "one of the most important and exciting campaigns I have ever undertaken."

With him he took 40 hand-picked Apache police; 60 more police — Naiche was said to be among them — under Chief of Apache Police Clay Beauford joined him at Silver City, New Mexico. Due to the rough terrain, the Apaches had to resole their moccasins every four days.

As they neared the agency, Clum and 22 of the police, whom he had mounted with horses at Silver City, double-timed

AGENT JOHN CLUM WITH APACHE POLICE

it to Warm Springs, arriving on the evening of April 20. The balance with Beauford, still on foot, followed at a slower pace.

A scout reported that "Geronimo, with 100 followers, was then camped about 3 miles from the agency, and that he had come into the agency that day for rations."

Meanwhile, three cavalry companies under Gen. Edward Hatch, commander of the Department of New Mexico, had been sent to aid Clum. They planned to reach the agency on April 21. When Clum received word that the cavalry wouldn't arrive until April 22, he feared the Apaches would bolt if he waited. Clum ordered Beauford to bring his force up quickly and quietly under cover of darkness.

When Beauford arrived at 4 A.M., Clum hid his men in the

commissary, one of several buildings that lined the agency's parade ground. As dawn streaked the New Mexico sky, Clum sent Geronimo a message that he wanted a conference with him and the other Apache leaders.

Geronimo later said, "The messengers did not say what they wanted with us, but as they seemed friendly, we thought they wanted a council and rode in to meet the officers."

Not suspecting a trap, the Apaches brought their women and children.

Clum positioned himself, Beauford, and six police on the administration building porch, facing the parade ground. Clum deployed the balance of the police "in an irregular skirmish line," on both sides of the parade ground.

In Clum's words, the Chiricahuas "came quickly, a motley clan, painted, and equipped for fight." Geronimo and six other leaders led the way.

"Sullen and defiant, they gathered in a compact group in front of me," Clum recalled.

He spoke first, accusing the Apaches of killing whites and Mexicans and stealing livestock. He chastised Geronimo for breaking his promise the year before to bring his people to San Carlos. Now, Clum said, he would take them to San Carlos.

Defiant, Geronimo growled, "We are not going to San Carlos with you, and unless you are very careful, you and your Apache police will not go back to San Carlos either. Your bodies will stay here at Ojo Caliente to make food for coyotes."

Surprised at how quickly the showdown had come, Clum took Geronimo's threat seriously. He later admitted that although he disliked the military, he had prayed for General Hatch's cavalry to ride up at that moment.

As Geronimo glared, Clum touched his hat, a signal to the Apache police in the commissary. The doors burst open and they poured out, rifles at the ready, and lined up along the south side of the parade ground. The Apaches found themselves trapped in a potential crossfire between the commissary and administration building. Some Apaches on the edge of the group started to slip away, but Beauford raised his rifle, halting them.

Clum later recounted, "I was watching Geronimo's face, and particularly the thumb of his right hand, which was about an inch back of the hammer of his .50-caliber United States Army Springfield rifle." It began "creeping slowly toward the hammer of his rifle."

Beauford awaited another signal.

"My right hand was resting on my right hip, akimbo fashion, and not more than an inch away from the handle of my Colt .45," Clum recalled. "I moved my right hand over until it touched the handle of my revolver. That was the second signal."

Beauford and the Apache police raised their rifles, each covering Geronimo or one of his "most notorious followers." Geronimo's thumb moved away from the hammer.

At this moment of high tension, an Apache woman dashed from the crowd, throwing herself on Beauford's back and wrapping her arms around his neck and shoulders. She tugged at his gun.

"Beauford was a powerful man," Clum recalled. "He gave one very disgusted look at the woman who had captured him, released his right arm, grabbed her around her waist, and gave a mighty heave. The lady landed down-side-up in the dust, about 10 feet away."

Beauford immediately leveled his rifle at Geronimo. By this time all the Apache police had emerged and stood in place. Geronimo knew he was beaten.

"It is well," he said. "We have been on the warpath a long time and are tired. If you want to have big smoke and big talk — we are ready."

This pleased Clum, but he said, "We cannot have the big smoke and big talk until we put away our firearms." He handed his rifle and pistol to one of the police and ordered the Apache leaders to lay down their weapons. They refused, shuffling their feet in the dirt of the parade ground.

Clum stepped from the porch and said, "I'll take your gun, myself." As he grasped Geronimo's rifle, he felt brief resistance before Geronimo released it. (Clum kept this souvenir of

Geronimo's only capture and passed it down through his family. Today the Arizona Historical Society Museum stores it in Tucson.)

"I have seen many looks of hate in my long life, but never one so vicious, so vengeful," Clum later wrote. Beauford disarmed the rest of the leaders. The other Apaches laid their rifles down.

Clum invited the leaders onto the porch for a conference while the other Apaches huddled or lay on the ground. The leaders squatted as Clum again chastised Geronimo for his deception of the previous year. He then told the leaders they were prisoners and ordered them to the guardhouse, forgetting that the Warm Springs agency didn't have one. When Geronimo remained squatting, Clum said, "You must go now."

Geronimo leaped to his feet. The other leaders and most of the warriors on the parade ground jumped to their feet. Geronimo's hand inched toward the knife at his waist. Clum watched his eyes and saw indecision; should he fight, probably to the death, or surrender? Before he could decide, one of the Apache police grabbed his knife from its sheath. The other police drew back the hammers of their rifles, creating a resounding click. For a moment Geronimo glared, and then relaxed, saying, "*Enju* [All right]."

Clum now had the problem of what to do with them without a guardhouse. To Beauford he said, "I think our guests will feel more secure if we rivet ankle-irons on them, and it might be well to permit their followers to witness the operation."

The police herded the leaders to the blacksmith shop, where they shackled Geronimo first with shackles made of wagon tires. After shackling the leaders, the police took them to the barbed wire-enclosed corral, which Clum described as "horse high and bull strong." He gave them hay for beds, blankets, and food, and placed them under guard — 10 police served two-hour tours inside the fence.

Beauford and 20 Apache police took the rest of the band to their camp, where they gathered their belongings and stolen livestock. They returned by sunset.

The next morning when Victorio rode to the agency to assess the situation, he learned just how much trouble Geronimo and the other Chiricahuas could cause him and his people.

Clum ordered him to bring all his people in for counting. Victorio's Warm Springs band numbered 343, Geronimo's Chiricahuas, 110.

The next day, Clum received a telegram from the commissioner of Indian Affairs ordering him to escort the Warm Springs Apaches to San Carlos as well.

The 453 Apaches and their escort reached San Carlos on May 20, 1877. Clum locked 19 of them in the guardhouse. The hanging of the leaders topped his to-do list.

Thinking some semblance of a trial was required, Clum wrote Sheriff Charles Shibell in Tucson, "Through my Apache police, and information they have obtained by fraternizing with the renegades, ample evidence is now available to convict each of the seven chiefs on many counts of murder."

The sheriff took no action.

Now, Clum again found himself embroiled in conflict with the Army. When he returned to the reservation with his prisoners, he found the Army had been ordered to "inspect and manage" the Indians at San Carlos. Furious, he wrote the commissioner of Indian Affairs in Washington, "If your department will increase my salary sufficiently and equip two more companies of Indian police for me, I will volunteer to take care of all Apaches in Arizona — and the troops can be removed."

When the commissioner dismissed his proposal, Clum resigned in a huff. Beauford also resigned in disgust.

Within two weeks after Clum resigned in July 1877, his successor unshackled Geronimo and those held with him and set them free. The sheriff had no interest in them.

Clum later said that Geronimo's shackles "never should have been removed, except to permit him to walk untrammeled to the scaffold," and that a "vast amount of expense, tribulation, distress and bloodshed" could have been avoided if Geronimo's arrest "had been swiftly followed by prosecution, conviction, and execution."

Clum's son, Woodworth, wrote in the book *Apache Agent*, "The inescapable fact is that had Geronimo been hanged in July 1877, if John P. Clum had been kept on his job at old San Carlos, the Apache wars would have been over in 1877, instead of 1886."

Many of the Apaches under Victorio remained bitter for the rest of their lives. In 1955, one told Geronimo biographer Angie Debo, "We were innocent and should not have been driven from our homes. We were not to blame for what Geronimo did. The United States didn't give this land to us. It was ours."

Geronimo himself understood how close he had come to death. Of his one and only capture and subsequent imprisonment, he said it "might easily have been death to me."

CHAPTER SEVEN

Wyatt Earp Chases Geronimo

Geronimo versus Wyatt Earp.
What a dream billing! While they never met,
their paths did cross once.

IN LATE SUMMER 1881, GERONIMO, JUH, AND THEIR BANDS were living quietly on the San Carlos Apache reservation. Now a farmer, Geronimo said he grew "corn in straight rows, the beans among the corn, and the melons and pumpkins in irregular order over the field."

Then the Army's arrest and killing of charismatic medicine man Noch-ay-det-klinne, known as The Prophet, and the subsequent bloody battle at Cibecue Creek in the White Mountains rocked the peace on the reservation.

Even though the agent, the corrupt Joseph Capron Tiffany, whom the Apaches called "Big Belly," said the Indians at San Carlos were "perfectly quiet during the whole White Mountain [Cibecue] trouble," the resultant tumult caused the Chiricahuas to fear their past sins might catch up with them.

The chaos settled into a rolling tremor, but the entire southwest remained on edge. In the middle of September, 22 companies of reinforcements from California and New Mexico arrived on the reservation to help quell any budding problems. This show of force made the Apaches more uneasy. Geronimo, Juh, and other Chiricahua Apaches approached Tiffany and asked him the meaning of the hordes of soldiers. He said he "told them to have no fear, that none of the Indians who had been peaceable would be molested in any way." They then asked him if the troops had anything to do with their warpath days in Mexico.

"I assured them it had not," said Tiffany. "They shook hands, much delighted, and went back."

On September 30, ration day on the reservation, three companies of soldiers rode onto the agency grounds to arrest two Apaches, Bonito and George, for their involvement in the Cibecue affair. This set into motion a series of events that rocked not only Arizona Territory but the entire Southwest as well.

Bonito and George bolted, but not before warning the Chiricahuas that "the soldiers were coming and would murder their women and children." Now certain they would at the very least be arrested, Geronimo, Juh, and the previously peaceful Naiche set out for Mexico with 74 warriors and approximately 400 women and children.

The dreaded message flew across Arizona Territory: The Apaches are out!

They headed south, slicing telegraph wires, killing whites, and stealing guns, ammunition, and more than $20,000 worth of horses. They fought battles with U.S. soldiers at Cedar Springs and in the Dragoon Mountains, delaying tactics that allowed their women and children to forge ahead, then slipped away and continued southward. Their route took them within 6 to 8 miles of Tombstone, whose mayor was John Clum, Geronimo's nemesis and the only man ever to capture him.

"I was sitting in my office in Tombstone," Clum remembered, when a courier rode up and down the street calling "Indians are coming."

Clum called a meeting of the Citizens' Home Guard to organize a posse. He chose 35 men, "equipped with rifles, six-shooters, ammunition, saddlebags, and canteens." They included Wyatt Earp and two of his brothers, Morgan and Virgil (Tombstone's chief of police), and Sheriff John Behan. The group voted Behan as captain and Virgil Earp as lieutenant.

"Remember, men," Clum told them, "no quarter, no prisoners. I delivered Geronimo to the Army once, in irons. They

CHIRICAHUA APACHE BONITO, 1883

turned him loose. If we get him this time, we will send him back to the Army, nailed up in a long narrow box, with a paper lily on his chest."

They dashed into the countryside. "We cut the fresh trail left by Geronimo and his renegades, and had quickened our pace in the hope of closing up with them by nightfall, or at least surprising them before they broke camp the next morning," Clum later wrote. As they reached Antelope Pass, a torrential desert thunderstorm broke loose. "Our clothing was soaked through to the skin, boots were full of water, and the soft ground was very tiring to our horses, although we could go no faster than a walk." They trudged on, following the Apaches' trail.

By midnight the rain had ceased and the weary posse, whose number had dwindled to 22, stopped at a small shack to rest themselves and their horses, and to dry out. At 2 A.M. the moon rose, and they started out once more.

"It hurt to sit again upon those sore spots, aggravated by wet saddles and wetter clothes," Clum wrote. "But none uttered the slightest protest. We were after Geronimo."

At noon, "We crossed the international line, were trespassing in Mexico, had seen no Apaches," even though the Indians traveled with women and children, recalled Clum. "We had no right to invade Mexico; were not equipped for an indefinite campaign; were out of grub; so we headed our horses northward, toward the U.S.A."

One of the posse, George Parsons, wrote, "It is better probably that we did not have a fight as their buffalo guns are longer ranged than ours."

Four companies of soldiers, also on Geronimo's trail, had stopped to wait out the storm. Clum's posse passed them as they prepared to resume their chase. Parsons said, they "moved leisurely off, bugles blowing an hour beforehand so as to notify all Indians to get out of the way."

Thus, Wyatt Earp lost his chance for an encounter with Geronimo, probably to Earp's benefit. And Clum lost the opportunity to recapture — or kill — his old enemy.

Geronimo would remain free in the Sierra Madre for more than two years before again returning to the reservation. Less than a month later the Earp brothers would meet the Clantons and the McLaurys at the O.K. Corral.

CHAPTER EIGHT

Rescuing Loco

Geronimo determined to "rescue" Loco
and his Warm Springs band
from the San Carlos Reservation —
whether they wanted to go or not.

———➤◆➤———

I N THE AFTERMATH OF THE 1881 CIBECUE MASSACRE, Geronimo, Juh, and Naiche jumped the San Carlos Reservation with their bands and escaped to the fastness of Mexico's Sierra Madre. However, Loco, chief of the Warm Springs Apaches, opted to stay on the reservation.

Four times during the next several months, Geronimo sent word to Loco that he must join his people in Mexico. Four times Loco rejected the demands. Geronimo, grumbling, decreed, "Loco belongs with his people," and determined to "rescue" him.

Although Geronimo wanted to save Loco and his people from the scanty rations and the scorching summer heat, he had another reason. "The Mexicans were gathering troops in the mountains where we were ranging," Geronimo said in his autobiography, "and their numbers were so much greater than ours."

The Apaches simply needed more men.

I n early April 1882, Geronimo, Naiche, the woman warrior Lozen, and possibly Juh, led a party of 76 warriors out of Mexico, bent on liberating Loco and his people.

Word of the Apaches' impending arrival reached the agency. A reliable informant wired from Corralitos, Chihuahua: "Ju [sic], Apache Chief, here. Think he will go for San Carlos." The military deployed troops into the field to keep "a closer

CHIEF LOCO OF THE WARM SPRINGS APACHES

and more vigorous watch" for any Apaches crossing the border.

The military's knowledge of their arrival presented no impediment for the Apaches. Breaking into groups of three or four, they moved through the desert like wraiths, slipping through the mountains in western New Mexico, and into Arizona via the Steins Peak Range. While scouting in this range, the Army's chief of scouts, Al Sieber, sent word that he had "discovered fresh Indian signs of the Chiricahuas making their way toward the San Carlos Agency." By the time the Army received his message, it was too late.

As the Apaches reached the San Simon River just north of Fort Bowie, two of Geronimo's warriors captured two choice horses and decided to take them back to Mexico. A small incident with tragic repercussions, for no one knew that Mexican soldiers then captured the warriors and demanded information on Geronimo's return route in exchange for their lives.

Meanwhile, the small parties formed into one cohesive band and continued northward. They stopped at the George Stevens ranch, where they slaughtered sheep, a pony belonging to Stevens' son, and all the Mexican hands.

As they neared the reservation, Geronimo sang four songs,

calling on his Power to bring success and to bring a deep sleep upon Loco, his people, and those at the agency.

During the evening of April 18, 1882, the Apaches from Mexico infiltrated the reservation, cutting the telegraph wires. Geronimo sent messengers to alert confederates of his arrival.

Jason Betzinez, a member of Loco's band, recalled sitting in a tent when hoof beats announced a visitor's arrival. He wrote in *I Fought with Geronimo*: "Outside someone spoke in Apache asking for Gil-lee." Betzinez ran out and directed the stranger. As the man left, he told Betzinez, "Don't be alarmed. We only want to see Gil-lee." But, Betzinez said, "We were alarmed. We knew that the man was a wild Indian from Mexico — a Nednhi. This made us afraid, for we knew that these outlaws had not come for any peaceful purpose."

Geronimo and his warriors hid in the scanty brush across the Gila River from Loco's camp. As dawn broke on April 19, they crossed the river, yelling and screaming. Someone, possibly Geronimo, yelled, "Take them all! Shoot down anyone who refuses to go with us! Some of you men lead them out."

Betzinez gave this account:

> We saw a line of Apache warriors spread out along the west side of camp and coming our way with guns in their hands. Others were swimming horses across the river or pushing floating logs ahead of themselves. The suddenness of this attack, its surprise effect, and the inhumane order from one of the chiefs calling for the shooting of people of his own blood threw us all into a tremendous flurry of excitement and fear.

At gunpoint, Geronimo forced Loco to lead the evacuation of 300 of his people, while he guided them east along the foothills north of the Gila. The fleeing Apaches heard shots from the vicinity of their rear guard. Warriors rode up with boots belonging to Albert D. Sterling, the chief of police. He and one of his Apache police, Sagotal, had ridden out to check on Loco's camp. The rear guard killed both men.

Loco slumped, resigned to his fate. Now that they had killed a white man, he and his people were outlaws. "We were filled the gloom and despair," Betzinez said. "What had we done to be treated so cruelly by members of our own race?"

They walked for many miles along the Gila River and then turned into the Gila Mountains. By sunset, Loco's people were exhausted and hungry. After resting briefly near a spring, Geronimo called for a night march.

Around midnight they stopped to rest by a spring. Geronimo called a council to discuss plans, rightfully including Loco, a great warrior and leader. At the same time, Geronimo sent warriors to a nearby sheep camp. They returned at sunrise, driving several hundred sheep.

"We were allowed to camp here for two days, gorging ourselves on good roast mutton and resting up for the next stage of the journey," Betzinez recalled.

Because this large group moved slowly and soldiers were scouring the countryside for them, Geronimo sent warriors out to capture horses and mules.

While the band waited behind a hill for these warriors, a young woman began her menses.

"Since this is one of the most important events in a woman's life the ceremony is never neglected, not even at a time such as this," Betzinez said. While they held a shortened, but no less solemn, puberty ceremony for her, shooting was heard over the hill where the warriors were raiding.

They broke the horses to ride and improvised saddles, according to Betzinez, "by wrapping cloth or skins around bundles of tules or reeds and tying them over the back of the animals."

The next evening, they began another night march. "All through the night we rode close together, so that no one would stray away from the columns," recalled Betzinez. "Now and then we could hear the voices of the wild Indians on all sides of us as they called softly to each other." The next morning, exhausted and disheartened, they stopped in the Steins Peak Range.

Lt. Col. George A. Forsythe of the 4th Cavalry, who was

searching for the Apaches, said of this range, "I never saw a more rugged place." At Horseshoe Canyon he cut the trail of Geronimo's scouts and sent his scouts to intercept them. Geronimo's scouts ambushed Forsythe's. The skirmish escalated to a full-blown battle as six cavalry troops joined the fray.

Although Forsythe, whom Al Sieber called faint-hearted and the Apaches called "Always Too Late to Fight," claimed to have won the battle, and probably could have, his troops killed only one Apache.

Geronimo called for yet another night march. As sunrise approached, the Apaches needed to cross San Simon Valley without being seen. He called on his Power to delay the sunrise. A warrior who witnessed this recalled, "So he sang, and the night remained for two or three hours longer. I saw this myself."

After another night march, the Apaches entered Mexico. Behind they left chaos — more than 50 whites killed, looted and burned freight wagons, and ranches divested of livestock.

Now that they had crossed the border, everyone, including the captive Apaches, relaxed. They felt no real threat from the Mexican soldiers, and "we began to feel safe from attack by U.S. troops," Betzinez said. The next night they came to the Janos Plains. "So we rode along across the plains, talking, laughing, and singing love songs in low voices — songs our people have long known and liked."

By the next morning, they had reached a small, rough mountain 25 miles north of Janos. Called Sierra Emmedio, it boasted a splendid spring. They decided to rest for a few days. The women cut mescal heads, which they buried in pits in the ground to slowly bake. This delighted the captives, who hadn't had this treat while on the reservation. "For two days and nights we gave ourselves up to merriment and dancing," Betzinez said. And they relaxed their guard.

Unknown to them, Forsythe had disobeyed international law and entered Mexico. Another officer, Capt. Tullius C.

Tupper of the 6th U.S. Cavalry, had crossed the border before Forsythe. He led a smaller force — 39 troopers and 47 Apache scouts under the command of Al Sieber.

On April 27, as it grew dark, Tupper spotted the fires of the Apaches' camp only 5 miles ahead. Sieber took four scouts and crept up to the camp, then reported back to Tupper. The captain decided his troops would attack from the plain while the scouts would position themselves on a ridge overlooking the Apaches' camp. As dawn broke on April 28, the scouts moved onto the ridge just as four Apaches approached their position.

Loco's grandson, Gooday; Gooday's mother; and two young girls had left the dancing that had continued throughout the night to check the mescal. One girl bent over the pit to pull out a mescal head. A shot rang out, and she sprawled across the pit. The other girl ran, and the scouts shot her. The revelers screamed. Gooday pulled his mother behind a rock.

Shocked and disoriented, the Apaches grabbed a few supplies as they fled to a rocky hill a short distance away. "All our people took cover in the broken ground at the butte, sometimes several trying to squeeze into the same crevice in the rocks," remembered Betzinez. "This was the worst thing that could have happened to us. We had nothing except our bare hands and the clothes on our backs."

As they ran, the warriors fired at the soldiers, but in their haste fired high and did little damage. The women and children hid in the rocks while the warriors continued to fire at the soldiers. They tried to rescue their horses, but the soldiers had already herded them off.

Back in the bosom of his tribe, "Loco tried to get the scouts to turn against us," Sieber said, "but they would abuse and curse him and fire into the rocks where he was." One bullet hit him in the leg.

An old woman thought her son, a scout named Tocklanny, rode with the troops. She "climbed up to the highest point of the butte where she stood in plain sight calling out to her son," yelling that they had been taken against their will, Betzinez recounted. A soldier's shot sent her cartwheeling to her death.

The two sides kept firing at each other, but inflicting little damage. Sieber said, "If the hostiles had kept cool, there would have been no chance at all and every man would have been shot down. As it was, they fired too high, and the bullets passed over our heads every time."

Early in the afternoon, four warriors circled behind the scouts on the ridge and fired on them, creating a diversion that allowed the rest of the Apaches to escape into the foothills. The scouts fired back and left their positions, rejoining Tupper's troops still firing from the plain.

Exhausted, out of ammunition, and outnumbered by the Apaches, Tupper's troops herded the Apaches' horses before them as they retreated 9 miles to their camp of the previous evening. Tupper later reported, "We could not get the savages out of the rocks and determined that no good could result from further firing." Here Forsythe's large contingent joined them.

Now in desperate straits, the Apaches had lost 14 warriors and many more were wounded. All of their supplies had been lost; they had grabbed only a little food as they ran from the camp. Warriors recaptured a few horses, but most went on foot. A much different band continued its journey across the Janos Plain than had joyfully started across it a few nights before.

By midnight they begged to stop and rest. Chief Naiche, on horseback, wanted to continue, but Geronimo insisted they stop. Irritated that Geronimo had countermanded his order, Naiche went on ahead with about a dozen warriors.

After a short rest, the Apaches resumed their march. When dawn broke, they had traveled 29 miles. Their column stretched for 2 miles along the dry streambed of Aliso Creek. The blue outline of their beloved Sierra Madre materialized against the morning sky. In a matter of hours they would be safely in the foothills.

A few warriors led the struggling group, but stopped to rest and smoke, while a larger contingent guarded the rear, protecting against a possible attack by the U.S. soldiers. The

Apaches walking at the front of the column smelled coffee, but they went on, thinking it came from their own people. They never suspected they smelled Mexican coffee. Nor did they suspect the two Apaches the Mexicans had captured while returning to Mexico with their horses had given Col. Lorenzo Garcia the Apaches' return route.

"A shot was fired. The women and children turned back, for the men were in the rear," said James Kaywaykla, who'd been a young boy in Nana's band. He wrote of his and others' experiences in the book *In the Days of Victorio*. Although not at Aliso Creek, he heard the story from those who were. Some 250 Mexican soldiers of the 6th Mexican Infantry under Garcia poured from a ravine and attacked the column.

Betzinez described what happened next:

> Almost immediately Mexicans were right among us all, shooting down women and children right and left. People were falling and bleeding, and dying, on all sides of us. Whole families were slaughtered on the spot.

Many escaped, Betzinez, his mother, and his sister among them. As they ran, Betzinez said, they heard Geronimo "calling to the men to gather around him and make a stand to protect the women and children."

Thirty-two warriors heeded his call. Others didn't. As Betzinez and his family fled toward the rendezvous spot, they saw Mangus, the son of Mangas Coloradas, and his small band, and Naiche and the warriors who had ridden ahead, smoking under a tree. These warriors had seen the Mexican soldiers, but had gone on without reporting it to those behind them. And they had heard gun fire, but elected not to help their own people. Betzinez called their actions a "disgraceful abandonment of their mission as a security detachment," and said, "I felt dreadfully ashamed of them."

Meanwhile, the battle raged at the ravine, where Garcia concentrated his attack. Geronimo, his 32 warriors, and the women and children had thrown themselves into the dry creek bed. They began firing at the Mexicans who made pass after pass, trying to dislodge them. The women dug holes in the walls where they placed their children for protection. The men dug toe holds so they could step up and fire. They dug into the sandy creek bottom and found water, which soon mixed with the blood of the wounded and dying.

"About noon," Geronimo recalled, "we began to hear them speaking my name with curses." The Mexican general called his officers aside for a meeting. Geronimo crawled close to listen. He later gave this account:

> I could hear all he said and I understood most of it. "Officers, yonder in those ditches is the red devil Geronimo and his hated band. This must be his last day. Kill men, women, and children; take no prisoners; dead Indians are what we want. Do not spare your own men; exterminate this band at any cost."

Both sides fought with a fierce determination. Ammunition began to run low. A bag of it lay some 50 feet away. Now deeply in league with his fellow warriors, Loco tried to reach it, but fire from the Mexicans sent him back to the arroyo. A woman, either Lozen or an old woman, depending on the report, ran out in a blaze of bullets and, with covering fire by Geronimo's brother, Fun, retrieved the bag.

Fun was the hero of the battle. He was said to have power over bullets and could dodge them. Three times he jumped out of the arroyo and ran, zigzagging, toward the Mexican soldiers, firing and reloading with bullets he held between his fingers.

As dusk came, the smell of smoke permeated the area. Geronimo recalled that "a dozen Indians had crawled out of the ditches and set fire to the long prairie grass behind the Mexican troops."

Others claim the Mexicans tried to burn the Apaches out. No matter who lit the grass, under the thick pall of smoke, the Apaches crept out of the creek bed.

Gooday, a Geronimo-hater his entire life, later related a strange story. He said Geronimo, who had been protecting the women and children all day, called to the warriors, "If we leave the women and children, we can escape." Aghast, Fun asked Geronimo to repeat his order. He did. Fun raised his rifle and said. "Say that again and I'll shoot you down right here." Geronimo supposedly disappeared over the top.

Gooday's account was so out of character for Geronimo, known for protecting his people, that its truthfulness is uncertain.

Survival was paramount to the Apaches, however. They sometimes made extreme sacrifices. While Fun held off the Mexicans until all the women and children in his sector had escaped, some groups did abandon babies. In other cases, Betzinez said, "The warriors asked the consent of the women to let them choke the infants so they wouldn't give away their movement by crying." They gave their permission. One woman reportedly strangled her own infant rather than chance it growing up in Mexican captivity.

Betzinez reported that for those who had congregated at the mountain rendezvous spot, "The night air was very cold at that altitude. We had lost all our blankets, and it was unsafe to build fires. Nevertheless by gathering grass and covering ourselves with it, we managed to sleep with a fair degree of comfort." The wounded suffered with no help. All night the wails of the grieving Apaches rang in the hills.

The next morning, the Apaches saw Forsythe's forces approaching Garcia's down on the plain. The Apaches anticipated a battle between the two. But nothing happened.

Garcia asked Forsythe by whose authority he had entered Mexico, then ordered him to leave. Forsythe, although under orders not to invade Mexican territory, said he had orders to eradicate the Apaches. Garcia then escorted him to view the previous day's battle site, strewn with Mexican and Apache corpses. The Mexican soldiers had killed most of the Apaches in the frenzied first onslaught. Loco's daughter had been taken captive. Three of Garcia's officers lay among the dead.

CHIEF NANA OF THE WARM SPRINGS APACHES

Sieber reported, "As far as I was able to see there were 11 bucks and plenty of squaws and children killed, and 14 squaws and 11 children captured. The Mexicans had 23 killed and about 30 wounded."

Garcia invited the Americans to breakfast, but upon finding the Mexican soldiers destitute, with no ammunition, food, clothing, or medical care, Forsythe instead offered his own hospitality. Garcia accepted. Forsythe also provided medical attention for the wounded soldiers. The two officers parted amicably, although Garcia gave Forsythe a written reprimand.

The decimated Apache band, huddled in the hills, listened as the peeling church bells in Janos tolled Garcia's victory.

Geronimo and those involved in the battle at Aliso Creek arrived a bit later. After greetings, while those warriors who had refused to help stood by silently, Geronimo ordered his depleted band to continue their trek. They traveled slowly as they had many wounded. Three days after fighting Tupper at Sierra Emmedio, Geronimo sent warriors out to capture some cattle, and the Apaches ate their first substantial meal since the night before Tupper's attack. After resting for two days, they kept on to Juh's camp deep in the Sierra Madre. They exchanged tearful greetings with friends and family not seen for many years. Juh's band "gave us food and blankets and by talking to us cheerfully tried to take our minds off our losses," Betzinez said.

Kaywaykla overheard Loco tell Nana that "costly as the fight had proved, a summer at San Carlos would have been more disastrous."

Forsythe's report of his Mexico excursion never made it to Washington. His commanding officer told him, "[T]he less said about it the better." Tupper's report, on the other hand, relocated his battle to the mountains of New Mexico, on the proper side of the international border.

While Geronimo's anger and determination to "rescue" Loco from the reservation ended in tragedy, the Apaches gathered in the fastness of the Sierra Madre included the best of their warriors. According to Betzinez, 80 were "first-line warriors" and another 50, "big boys ready to fight." Close to 500 or 600, they represented a larger number of Apaches than had gathered together in years.

CHAPTER NINE

The Stevens Ranch Massacre

A meal at gunpoint with Geronimo's raiders suddenly turned deadly.

After jumping the San Carlos reservation in 1881, Geronimo and his band lived in the Sierra Madre in Mexico. In mid-April 1882, he returned to Arizona Territory to "rescue" Chief Loco and his Warm Springs band, who had chosen to stay on the reservation.

On their way to Loco's camp on the reservation, Geronimo and his warriors came to Ash Flat, about 20 miles north of Safford, Arizona, and a sheep ranch owned by the Graham County sheriff, George Stevens. Although the Stevens family wasn't there, their Apache and Mexican ranch hands were.

The foreman, Victoriano Mestas, knew Geronimo. While Mestas was a child in Mexico, Geronimo had killed his mother, father, and his two sisters and captured him. Geronimo had treated him well, as the Apaches did with adopted children. He gave him a pony with a saddle to ride and fed and clothed him. Eventually, he had traded Mestas to a white rancher. When grown, Mestas had reverted to his Mexican heritage and married a Mexican woman. Under his charge at the ranch were 10 Mexican and three White Mountain Apache ranch hands who cared for the herd of 10,000 sheep.

An Apache hand named Bylas was related to Steven's Apache wife. His family, the families of the other Apache herders, Mestas' wife and three children, and two other Mexican women were also in camp.

Those at the ranch witnessed the frightening sight of 76 Apache warriors, riding five or six abreast, descending upon them with Geronimo, Naiche, Chatto (who would later scout for the Army), and Chihuahua leading the way.

The Apache raiders wanted food. They began slaughtering sheep, and Geronimo, who had a fondness for horsemeat, shot and killed a pony belonging to Jimmie Stevens, the owner's son.

"Your women will make tortillas and fix the pony meat," he ordered, "or I will kill all of you. If you feed us well, we will go on our way and not harm you."

The women, along with Bylas and two herders, hurriedly prepared a meal that the Apaches and Mexicans alike devoured. Afterward, everyone squatted in small groups in the shade.

Then came the first hint that something was amiss. Geronimo admired Mestas' expensive, elaborately embroidered shirt, then ordered him to remove it. Trembling, Mestas obeyed. Geronimo rolled it up and put it in his saddlebag. He raised his hand and war whoops split the air. The warriors began shooting, stabbing, and clubbing the Mexicans. According to the official report, it ended quickly. Mestas lay dead, as did his wife, two of their children, and all 10 of the Mexican herders. Only Bylas, his wife, and the Apache herders survived.

Almost. Mestas' 9-year-old son, Stanislaus, had hidden under Señora Bylas's skirts. When Geronimo discovered the boy, he prepared to kill him and the woman for hiding him. Naiche stepped forward, chastising Geronimo for being dishonorable. He forbade him to touch either of the Bylases or the boy, telling Geronimo he would kill him if he harmed them.

Young Stanislaus gave an eyewitness account via a Tucson dispatch, differing somewhat from other eyewitness reports:

> The Indians rushed in from all sides and overpowered [us]. An Indian put the muzzle of his gun against the head of one man and fired, blowing his brains against the floor and walls. I saw them kill my mother and two little brothers by beating their brains out with stones. They took my father and tortured him most

dreadfully. He begged them to spare him, but they only tortured him the more. When they were tired of torturing him, one of them split his head with an axe. An Indian squaw, wife of one of the four friendly Apache herders who worked with us, saved my life by holding me behind her and begging them to spare me.

Years later in Omaha at the Trans-Mississippi and International Exposition of 1898, Jimmie Stevens, whose pony Geronimo had killed and eaten at the ranch, came face to face with the aged warrior. Geronimo asked Stevens to interpret for him when he spoke with his old adversary, Gen. Nelson Miles, who was there celebrating Army Day.

"Yes," replied Stevens, "if you'll pay me for the sorrel colt you had killed and eaten at my father's sheep camp in 1882."

"How much do you want for the colt?" Geronimo asked.

"Fifty dollars," Stevens replied.

"It's too much for the colt," Geronimo said, "and besides, I don't have that much money."

"Geronimo never did pay me for that pony," Stevens recalled, "but it was worth $50 to look at his face when I interpreted for General Miles," during their acrimonious encounter.

CHAPTER TEN

Geronimo's Cattle

Geronimo and Lt. Britton Davis
play a little joke with 135 head
of stolen Mexican cattle.

———◆———

IN MAY 1883, GEN. GEORGE CROOK HAD TRACKED GERONIMO and his people to their lairs deep in the Sierra Madre. Geronimo promised to round up his far-flung people and bring them to the San Carlos Reservation in Arizona.

In October, Crook began to get antsy, wondering if the newspapers' tag of "Crook's folly" would prove true, if Geronimo had stood him up. Naiche, Chihuahua, and Chatto had all come in with their families, and Lt. Britton Davis had escorted them to the reservation. Others had made their way through the secret mountain trails and across the plains to the reservation. But not Geronimo. Crook sent Davis to the border with a pack train and a company of scouts to escort the errant Apache to the reservation and provide protection from the up-in-arms ranchers and miners if and when he appeared.

For weeks, Davis's scouts patrolled the border, watching for Geronimo and his band. Davis even had the Apache medicine man traveling with the scouts — Davis called him "my old friend" — perform a ceremony to find Geronimo. After hours of incantations, the medicine man pronounced, "Geronimo was three days away, riding on a white mule, and bringing a great lot of horses."

Davis hurried from San Bernardino Springs, where he had been camping, to the border, and there! A ragged line of Apaches straggled toward the border, including three of Geronimo's wives — She-gha, Zi-yeh, and Ih-tedda. A son had died on the trip. (Years later, in his book *The Truth About Geronimo*, Davis set the number of Apaches at 97, but his official dispatches at the time numbered them at only 32, including Geronimo.)

Because "they were as wary and suspicious as so many wild animals," Davis said, he sent two scouts to meet Geronimo below the border and explain that the soldiers were there simply as an escort.

His foul mood plainly showing, Geronimo rode his white pony up to Davis, checking it "only when its shoulder had bumped the shoulder of my mule," Davis recalled.

Geronimo said he had made peace with the whites. So why, he asked, was Davis there? Why was an escort needed?. Davis explained that he was concerned only about some white men, those who drank a lot of whiskey and might try to harm the Apaches. Geronimo grudgingly accepted Davis' explanation and shook his hand, Davis said, declaring "that he and I were thenceforth brothers."

Davis next turned his attention to a dust cloud, thinking Mexican soldiers were chasing the Apaches.

"*Gando*," Geronimo said. "Cattle." He had stolen 135 head of Mexican beeves, cows, and calves to provide bartering stock when he reached the reservation.

The herd alarmed Davis. Driving cattle meant the Apaches and soldiers had to travel slowly and follow the main routes, where they could find feed and water. The routes also exposed the Apaches to those who wished to harm them. But, recalled Kaywaykla, who was riding with the band, "Geronimo refused to go without them." Knowing that the least little dispute could send the Chiricahuas back into Mexico, Davis agreed to let Geronimo keep the herd.

Geronimo asked for three days rest. He had been pushing the cattle to outrun the Mexicans, and the animals needed to recoup. Davis agreed to one day. When Geronimo complained, Davis reminded him that the Mexicans could cross the border.

Davis recalled that Geronimo growled, "Mexicans! My squaws can whip all the Mexicans in Chihuahua."

But, Davis said, he, Geronimo, was low on ammunition.

Again Geronimo harrumphed, "I don't fight Mexicans with cartridges. I fight them with rocks and keep my cartridges to fight the white soldiers."

The next day they started, making 18 to 20 miles a day. Every evening Geronimo demanded a long rest, telling Davis that the fast pace was "running all the fat off the cattle and they would not be fit for trading when we reached the reservation." At Sulphur Springs, Geronimo made his stand. He would go no farther until his cattle had rested. If Davis wanted to go on ahead, fine, but he intended to rest his cattle for a few days. Davis again agreed to one day's rest.

They camped at a ranch with a small house enclosed by an adobe wall about 5 feet high. Before supper, two civilians strolled out of the ranch house. One flashed a badge and informed Davis he was the U.S. marshal for the Southern District of Arizona. The other claimed to be the customs collector from Nogales, Arizona Territory. They had come to arrest Geronimo and his warriors for the murder of Arizona citizens and to confiscate the cattle. The marshal told Davis, "I order you to arrest them and take them with their smuggled stock to Tucson for trial."

Not taking kindly to the two men, Davis replied that he obeyed orders only from General Crook.

"I am going to have those Indians," the marshal told Davis, "and then I am going to see that you answer to the federal court for your refusal to obey my order."

Davis fumed, but he stayed outwardly cool. He became even more determined to help Geronimo and his people keep their cattle. He had to find a way to convince Geronimo to get on the trail with his cattle without spooking him with news of the murder warrant.

Just then, a friend and fellow officer that Davis had invited to the ranch, J.Y.F. "Bo" Blake, rode in from Fort Bowie. Blake was Davis's superior officer, having graduated from West Point a year ahead of him. He ordered Davis to remain at the ranch. If Geronimo would move out with the cattle, Blake would accompany him.

WHITE MOUNTAIN APACHES SHUS-EL-DAY, SKRO-KIT, AND DAS-LUCA SERVED AS U.S. ARMY SCOUTS.

The challenge was to get Geronimo to move without alerting the two civilian authorities.

"The plan looked simple," Davis later wrote. "So does flying."

After supper, Davis and Blake joined the two civilians, offering to share the "quart of good Scotch whisky" that Blake had brought with him. In fact, they made sure the civilians drank most of it. The officials bade Davis and Blake goodnight.

The marshal bedded down on the porch, giving the two officers a moment of despair. Upon hearing their snores, though, Davis sent a scout to awaken Geronimo. Soon a group of scouts and warriors surrounded Geronimo, Davis, and Blake. Still not telling Geronimo about the murder charge hanging over his head, Davis said Geronimo should start immediately for the reservation, that the two men had come to collect $1,000 for the cattle. If Geronimo refused to pay, the civilian officials would simply take the livestock to Tucson for sale.

Geronimo faced Davis, anger sparking from every pore. He was going back to bed, he said. He had come in peace and had found nothing but trouble. Let them try to take his cattle. He intended to stay. "Then he contemptuously demanded to know why I had disturbed him for a trivial talk that meant nothing," recounted Davis.

A sergeant of scouts stepped up. "He was of a tribe hostile to the Chiricahua, and he hated Geronimo from the depths of his soul," Davis wrote.

The scout spoke rapidly to Geronimo. The situation became so tense that the interpreter, Mickey Free, dared not speak, so Davis never knew what the scout had said.

"Geronimo's feathers began to droop" before whatever logic he was hearing, Davis said. The lieutenant took advantage of the situation and Geronimo's immense pride. Knowing the Apaches "could leave me standing where I was and I would not know that they were gone," such was their skill at moving swiftly and silently and blending into the desert, Davis gibed that Geronimo and his people probably weren't smart enough to get away undiscovered anyway. Then he played to the Apaches' great sense of humor. What a good joke it would be, he said to Geronimo, if the two white men woke the next morning and the Apaches and all the cattle and ponies were gone.

Something close to a smile appeared on Geronimo's face.

Davis woke the packmaster and sent the pack train on its way. When he returned to the ranch house, every Apache had disappeared.

Kaywaykla, who understood some English and took the name James in captivity, later told the story from the Apaches' viewpoint: "One man said he was from the Customs and he wanted to take our cattle because we had not paid any tax on them. Our cattle! He hadn't stolen those cattle; why should he get them?"

Of Davis's goading Geronimo about being able to get away undetected, Kaywaykla said:

> If any people knows how to be quiet it is the Apache. We shook with laughter as we got everything ready to move. It did not take 10 minutes. Not a dog barked. Not a baby cried. We tied children's feet together under the bellies of the horses. We tied small children to adults. And we started. At first we moved slowly, very slowly. We had to, because of the cattle. But after we got out of hearing we put boys with lances to keep the cattle moving, and we made time. By morning we were far north of that spring.

Davis posted himself near the house. He sat on a box and held his mule's bridle in his hand. As the sun rose, the marshal, sleeping on the porch, stirred and sat up. He looked around. Stunned, he jumped up and called his friend. Still in their underwear and bare feet, the two men climbed to the roof of the house, scanning the countryside through binoculars. Not an Apache, not a single stray calf, not even a puff of dust could be seen. Other than the ranch cattle, Davis said, the only thing in sight was "a dejected-looking second lieutenant seated on a cracker box holding a sleepy-looking mule by the bridle."

The two angry men confronted Davis. He shook his head and shrugged his shoulders, explaining that during the night Blake, as his superior officer, had taken charge of the Apaches. He had moved them and the cattle out. Where he had taken them Davis didn't know, but he guessed they were at least 40 miles away by now.

"You are lying," the marshal said.

"Perhaps I am, but you can't prove it," Davis replied, smiling.

By riding hard, Davis caught up with Blake, the Apaches, and their cattle two days later not far from San Carlos. He delivered the entire bunch to reservation officials.

The story, however, did not end happily for Geronimo. While overlooking the stolen horses on which the Apaches rode, General Crook could not ignore the theft of more than 100 head of Mexican cattle. He confiscated them, sold them for $1,762.50, and turned the money over to the Mexican government.

Davis believed the cattle episode played a major part in a bitter, resentful Geronimo's breakout from the reservation a year later, and the beginning of what became known as the Geronimo Wars.

Geronimo never understood nor forgave Crook for what the Apache leader considered a breech of trust. Twenty years later Geronimo still complained:

> I told Crook that these were not white man's cattle, but belonged to us, for we had taken them from the Mexicans during our wars. I also told him that we did not intend to kill these animals, but that we wished to keep them and raise stock on our range. He would not listen to me, but took the stock.

CHAPTER ELEVEN

A Whiskey Peddler Prolongs the War

*One man's arrogant greed
sets the stage for monumental disaster.*

⇒•⇐

O N A SUNNY SUNDAY AFTERNOON IN MAY 1885, BRITTON Davis, then agent at Turkey Creek on the Fort Apache Reservation, was spending a pleasant day umpiring a baseball game. Two of his scouts, Chatto and Mickey Free, interrupted him with bad news. Some 143 Apache men, women, and children had jumped the reservation. The Apaches, including Geronimo, Naiche, Mangus, Old Nana, Lozen, and Chihuahua, were headed for Mexico.

All had seemed peaceful, but recently, Gen. George Crook had forbidden the Apaches to make and drink the fermented-corn drink *tizwin* or to beat their wives. This ban frustrated and irritated the Apaches, who considered both activities a part of their culture. Finally, breaking the ban with a rebellious night of drinking, the leaders appeared at Davis's tent to flaunt their crime. Unsure how to react, Davis told them he would have to inform Crook, but his telegram never reached the general.

While the Apaches waited for Crook's decree on their behavior, a rumor spread, which Geronimo later recalled: "The Americans were going to arrest me and hang me."

Days passed with no word. The Apaches became ever more antsy, and finally, on May 17, they bolted for Mexico, cutting telegraph wires, setting fires, and killing whites along the way. The whites weren't the only casualties. Soldiers found the bodies of two Apache newborns, infants discarded in the name of survival.

For months the rebel Apaches conducted deadly raids across the border, then fled back to Mexico. Arizona Territory quaked in fear and hate, its citizens crying for Apache blood.

The commander-in-chief of the U.S. Army, Gen. Philip A. Sheridan, and Crook decided to make a concerted attempt to break up the Apaches' base of operation in Mexico. They sent Capt. Wirt Davis (not to be confused with Lt. Britton Davis) and Capt. Emmett Crawford to lead the U.S. forces.

Setting out at twilight on January 3, 1886, Apache scouts led them into Mexico, Davis going one direction and Crawford another. On January 9, the scouts reported to Crawford that they had found the rebel Apaches' camp.

Fearful the Apaches would hear them coming, the scouts asked the soldiers to don moccasins. Early the morning of January 10, after an all-night trek, they surrounded the Apaches' camp. When a braying burro alerted the Apaches, Lt. Marion P. Maus, second in command to Crawford, said, "The hostiles, like so many quail, had disappeared among the rocks."

That afternoon, as Crawford's exhausted command rested in the Indian camp, Geronimo sent Lozen to him with a message. He wanted to parley.

But it was not to be.

The next morning, Mexican troops attacked the Americans, perhaps thinking they were Apaches. Crawford rushed forward, jumped on a rock, and waved a white handkerchief, shouting "*Soldados Americanos* [American soldiers]."

"One shot rang out, distinct and alone," Maus recalled. He turned and "found Crawford lying with his head pierced by a ball. His brain was running down his face and some of it lay on the rocks." Crawford would die seven days later.

Maus took command. Lozen and Tahdeste, the women Geronimo used to carry his messages, came into camp and arranged a meeting between Geronimo and the lieutenant.

After agreeing to meet with Crook in "two moons" to discuss a surrender, Geronimo turned over nine of his people to

GERONIMO (CENTER LEFT) AND GENERAL CROOK (SECOND FROM RIGHT) NEGOTIATE FOR SURRENDER.

Maus to take back to Fort Bowie. They included Old Nana, one of Naiche's wives, Geronimo's sickly daughter, and his Mescalero wife, Ih-tedda, who was pregnant.

True to his word, Geronimo and his band arrived at Cañon de los Embudos, about 25 miles south of the Mexican border on March 19, 1886. They set up camp, wrote Crook's aide, John G. Bourke, "in a lava bed, on top of a small conical hill surrounded by steep ravines not 500 yards in direct line from Maus, but having between the two positions two or three steep and rugged gulches which served as scarps and counter-scarps."

They now had several escape routes.

Crook arrived on March 24. With him came Tombstone photographer C.S. Fly, who took the only photos of Geronimo while he was a fugitive. Not only did Fly wander into the still-hostile Apaches' camp, but he posed them in groups, ordering them to move here or stand there. Geronimo, getting into the mood of it, even requested certain family groupings.

After Crook enjoyed a warm meal, the Apaches started

arriving. "Not more than half a dozen would enter camp at the same time," Bourke observed, describing their nervousness.

Crook described them as "fierce as so many tigers — knowing what pitiless brutes they are themselves, they mistrust everyone else."

Geronimo had, in fact, ordered his men to "kill all they could, and scatter in the mountains," at the slightest sign of treachery.

Geronimo and Naiche deliberated off to the side before sitting down with Crook. Geronimo claimed he "hadn't killed a horse or man, American or Indian," while living on the reservation. "I think I am a good man," he said, "but in the papers all over the world they say I am a bad man; but it is a bad thing to say so about me. I never do wrong without a cause."

Bourke noted that Geronimo appeared "nervous and agitated," that "perspiration in great beads, rolled down his temples and over his hands; and he clutched from time to time at a buckskin thong which he held tightly in one hand."

Reaching a fever pitch and disturbed that Crook seemed unimpressed by his words, Geronimo growled, "I want no more of this."

Crook had heard enough. He accused Geronimo of being a liar and, in so many words, a whiner. He issued an ultimatum. "You must make up your mind whether you will stay out on the warpath or surrender unconditionally. If you stay out, I'll keep after you and kill the last one, if it takes 50 years."

On March 27, the parties agreed on surrender terms. The Apaches would be sent to Florida for two years — although they had negotiated mightily to return to Fort Apache — and then they would be returned to Arizona Territory.

Geronimo sat cross-legged on the stream bank under a mulberry tree. His face, blackened with crushed galena, mirrored his mood. After Chihuahua and Naiche surrendered, Geronimo shook Crook's hand and said, ". . . Do with me what you please. I surrender. Once I moved about like the wind. Now I surrender to you and that is all."

**CHIEF NAICHE WITH ONE OF HIS WIVES,
WHO IS NOT IDENTIFIED ON THE ORIGINAL PHOTOGRAPH.**

Unhappy that they could not return to Fort Apache and feeling that Crook did not take their complaints seriously, the Apaches' mood turned ugly that night. Taking advantage of the Apaches unhappiness, a bootlegger named Charles F. Tribolet sneaked into the Apache camp after dark and sold them mescal. An observer told Bourke that Tribolet sold $30 worth of whiskey to the Apaches in an hour. He later boasted that he could have sold $100 worth at $10 a barrel if he had not been stopped.

A far worse crime, however, was his playing on the excitable and suspicious Apaches' fears. As he dispensed whiskey, Tribolet whispered that the soldiers would hang them as soon as they crossed the border from Mexico into Arizona Territory.

During that night, Maus recalled, "I could hear firing in their camp a mile or so away." Before daylight, scouts woke Crook with the news that Naiche "was so drunk he couldn't stand up and was lying prone on he ground."

Crook, whom General Sheridan had told, "the escape of the hostiles must not be allowed under any circumstances," left for Fort Bowie on March 28, leaving Maus to start the slow journey north with the Apaches. As he left, Crook saw evidence of the previous night's debauchery. Mules, still saddled, wandered aimlessly. Geronimo and four other warriors sat on two mules and were "drunk as lords," according to Bourke.

The skittish band, with Maus riding with them, moved slowly in small, scattered groups. They made little progress that day, camping at a supply camp that night. The next day, the March 29, Geronimo remained in a foul mood, dwelling on Tribolet's whispered warnings.

"I met Geronimo and a number of warriors gathered together nearby on Alias Creek, many of them being drunk," Maus remembered, "and Geronimo told me they would follow, but that I had better go on or he would not be responsible for my life." Maus sent a detail to destroy Tribolet's whiskey.

That night, while camped at San Bernardino Springs, the Apaches made their breakout plans. H.W. Daley, in charge of the Army pack train, said later, "There is no doubt that Geronimo made up his mind that night to play a trick on General Crook that he would never forget."

Tribolet had found more mescal and resumed his treacherous business. When Maus entered the Apaches' camp after they had stopped for the night, he found trouble: Naiche had shot his wife, E-clah-heh.

The generally accepted story is that E-clah-heh had tired of the hard life of running and hiding. When she learned of the planned breakout, she ran toward the soldiers' camp. Naiche shot her in the leg to stop her from revealing the plan.

Charles F. Lummis, a *Los Angeles Times* reporter based

at Fort Bowie during this time, sat in on the debriefing of some of the scouts. He heard a different story. Someone flirted with Naiche's wife, they claimed, and "jealous, Naiche shot the woman through the knee with a six-shooter."

Maus in his report said, "I found the trouble was over some women." Whatever the reason, E-clah-heh and a daughter remained with Maus.

During the cold, drizzling night, Maus heard shots fired. When he got up the next morning, he found that Geronimo and Naiche, along with 18 warriors (two later turned back and rejoined Maus), 14 women, and six children, had left during the night. They had taken only two horses and a mule.

Maus immediately started the remaining Apaches toward Fort Bowie under another officer, while he and the scouts tracked the fleeing Apaches into the Mexican mountains. The trail petered out at the Bavispe River. Not catching even a glimpse of the band, Maus turned back and returned to Fort Bowie.

At Fort Bowie, Crook told Lummis, "That man [Tribolet] is the cause of this whole trouble now." In retrospect, Crook said, it would have been preferable had some soldier "shot him down like a coyote, as he deserved to be."

Tribolet told Lummis that "it's money in my pocket to have those fellows out." He also bragged about how much whiskey he had sold them and even that he'd presented Geronimo with a bottle of champagne.

Years later, Geronimo and Naiche gave their reasons for leaving that night. Geronimo said in his autobiography:

We started with all our tribe to go with General Crook, but I feared treachery and decided to remain in Mexico. We were not under any guard at this time. The United States troops [mainly scouts] marched in front and the Indians followed, and when we became suspicious, we turned back.

Naiche's explanation was more ambiguous. When Crook visited the Apaches in Alabama in 1890, Naiche told him, "I was afraid I was going to be taken off somewhere I didn't like, to some place I didn't know. I thought all who were taken away would die."

"Didn't the Indians talk about it among themselves?" asked Crook.

"We talked to each other about it," replied Naiche. "We were drunk."

"Why did you get drunk?"

"Because there was a lot of whiskey there and we wanted a drink, and took it," the forthright chief said.

The March 5, 1888, edition of the *Chicago Tribune*, quoted Naiche as saying, "We saw that we were in for it and would be probably killed anyway, so we concluded to take our chances and escape with our lives and liberty."

No matter the reason, this idea planted in Geronimo's mind by an itinerant whiskey peddler cost the Apaches, the United States, and Mexico dearly. General Crook resigned in disgrace after Sheridan sent him a telegram, saying, "It seems strange that Geronimo and party could have escaped without the knowledge of the scouts." President Cleveland used Geronimo's outbreak as an excuse to nullify the concessions Crook had agreed to with the Apaches.

The *rurales*, the rural Mexican police, later shot and killed Tribolet when he tried to hold up a stagecoach in Mexico.

More than four months passed, along with a heavy loss of life and extensive military activity, before Naiche's and Geronimo's small band of 38 agreed to surrender — this time for good.

CHAPTER TWELVE

The Peck Ranch Massacre

*After Geronimo reneged on his surrender
at Cañon de los Embudos, Mexico,
his band skirmished with troops and raided
into Arizona continually. One April morning,
the Peck ranch lay in their path.*

———◦———

"THE DAY THE INDIANS RAIDED US, WE DIDN'T HAVE THE least idea there was an Indian anywhere near in the country," Arthur "Al" L. Peck recalled. "Charlie [Owens, his neighbor] and I had gone out to doctor some cattle. We were about a mile away from the house, and neither of us had any kind of gun on us."

Petra Peck, Peck's Mexican-born wife who was pregnant, was at their small, dirt-floored house with their 13-month-old daughter and Mrs. Peck's 10-year-old niece, Trinidad "Trini" Verdin. In recounting her story, Trini said that around 9 A.M., the Pecks' dog set up a howl. Thinking a coyote or some other creature skulked about, her aunt told her to "look out and see what the dog is barking at." Trini ran out and "saw an Apache sitting down near the corner of the corral."

Trini called a warning to Mrs Peck. Carrying the baby, Mrs. Peck rushed out the door. The Apache shot both her and the baby. He then called to several others who had hidden behind the corral.

Trini later said, "These other Apaches then came up and all of them ransacked the house and took me prisoner."

Trini rode behind the Indians' leader, whom she described from a 10-year-old's perspective as "A fat old man, short and thick-set and big-cheeked." Clearly, Geronimo.

Meanwhile, Peck and Owens had arrived at the field. Peck, dismounting, heard Owens cry, "Indians, Peck! For God's sake, run!"

Geronimo and his warriors, fresh from the bloodletting at the Peck ranch and whooping the distinctive Apache war cry, rode pell-mell toward the two men. Owens spurred his horse into a run, but bullets ripped through his body, and he fell, dead. Peck leaped back on his horse, but the Apaches shot it out from under him.

Geronimo rode up with Trini behind him. Dismounting, he walked toward Peck and motioned toward his boots. Peck sat down and removed them. Geronimo then demanded that Peck speak. Peck, who stuttered when stressed, could only utter strange sounds. Geronimo began backing up, saying "Go away," possibly thinking Peck was crazy.

During this time Peck remembered "seeing my wife's niece Trini, but they would not let me talk to her. She was crying."

Trini remembered that Peck "asked me where the baby was. I told him the baby was dead. The Apaches told me to shut up." She saw the Apaches let Peck go, although she was not sure why.

Nor was anyone else. Perhaps they believed him loco because he stuttered. Or perhaps they knew of the kindnesses he had done Apaches in the mines in Mexico years before. Whatever the reason, they rode off with Trini, and Peck began the long walk — barefooted — toward the town of Calabasas.

Although Peck had been told his wife and child were dead, he appeared to be in denial. T.D. Casanega, a member of the posse that formed to track down the marauders, later wrote, "Peck wanted us to go back and bring his wife and child a doctor."

After her rescue some weeks later, Trini gave two official reports — one, through an interpreter, to Lt. Leighton

**ARTHUR "AL" L. PECK SURVIVED
GERONIMO'S RAID, BUT HIS WIFE, BABY,
AND UNBORN CHILD DID NOT.**

Finley of the 10th Cavalry; and another, a week later, to J.A. Rivera, prefect at Magdalena, Sonora, who spoke with her in Spanish.

To Finley, she said that the Apache attackers numbered 30 to 40, clearly an exaggeration brought on by the horror of what she had just witnessed. Geronimo had only 17 warriors riding with him. Later, she told Rivera, "there were about 15 of them, that they did not have their women and families with them." When asked about the entire number in the party, he said she told him, "The entire band, men and women, amounted to about the same number as the force that rescued her, 30 men." All of the Apaches, including the children, carried rifles.

After Trini traveled with Geronimo and his warriors for about a week, women and children joined the band. During the time Trini rode with the Apaches, Geronimo and his wife She-gha cared for her, feeding her, she said, "beef, tortillas when they had flour, and coffee that they carried with them. Only rarely did they eat horse meat and that only when they had no beef."

When asked what mischief the Apaches had been up to, she told Rivera, "They have been keeping quiet. They have not attacked any point that I know of. This party was all mounted and always has been mounted."

But Rivera also reported that she "recalled them killing

two vaqueros near a railroad track and a few days later a little, old man cutting wood in a clump of trees." She also told Finley that "I saw, after they were dead, two Americans who had been killed by the Apaches, near Agua Fria."

Although some reports said Geronimo's warriors had raped Trini — typical of Apache reports at the time — she was not. In her reports to Finley and Rivera, Trini claimed only to have been badly treated by the Apaches. Details of how they mistreated her varied.

To Finley she said, "They have half-starved me and have beaten me. The old man I mentioned [Geronimo] gave me this blow between the eyes [showing an ugly bruise]. He would tell me in the Apache language to do something and I would not understand what he wished me to do, and then he would strike me."

She told Rivera "that they hit her a few times because she could not understand what they wanted her to do, but only the women hit her. She could not recall any man hitting her, though the men did scold her for stepping on the dirt instead of on the rocks and grass when they traveled afoot, so as to leave no footprint."

Trini was rescued by 30 Mexican cavalrymen led by Rivera. On June 17, they stopped in El Gusano, Sonora, around 2 P.M. to water their horses.

According to Rivera, they "unexpectedly came upon three Indians with their families and a herd of unbridled horses. The entire party was mounted on saddled horses. Our troops attacked and were able to recover all of their stolen property: saddles, valises of clothing, coffee pots, gunpowder, primers for remaking cartridges, a machine for this same purpose, and various other interesting items."

Geronimo and the other Apaches escaped into the rougher terrain of El Gusano Canyon, but not before the Mexicans killed a woman and wounded him. He started to fall from his saddle, then pulled himself back up. Trini, still riding behind him, fell to the ground, badly bruising herself. As Geronimo escaped, he called for Trini to follow him. Instead she ran toward the Mexicans from behind a rock where she had hidden, yelling, "Don't shoot. I'm Mexican."

A battle ensued, but when darkness fell, the Mexicans pulled out for lack of water. They suffered three men killed and one wounded. The woman killed at the outset was the Apaches' only loss. Trini told Rivera that she "also saw the soldiers scalp her."

The next day, Leonard Wood, an Army surgeon, came upon her body and helped bury her. Wood also reported that on June 18, his unit ran into a contingent of Mexican soldiers. With them was "the little Peck child," a reference to Trini.

In Geronimo's account of this period, less than three months before his fourth and final surrender, he said, "We ranged in the mountains of New Mexico for some time, then thinking that perhaps the troops had left Mexico, we returned. On our return through Old Mexico we attacked every Mexican found, even if for no other reason than to kill."

He mentions neither Peck nor Trini, nor even the raid on the ranch. To him it amounted to another day of survival.

Peck never returned to his ranch. He lived a long life, remarrying and raising a family. His daughter-in-law wrote, "Dad Peck never talked much of the Indian raid and we never pressed him for details, for even thinking of it upset him badly." Occasionally, he mentioned bits and pieces of the story to family members, which they wrote down.

No record traces Trini's movements after her rescue. Although some reports said Peck took her back to Arizona Territory, it's more likely she remained in Mexico with an aunt, Maria Cuen, her only living relative.

Geronimo and Gatewood

In a telling exchange between adversaries,
Geronimo asked the Army officer to think like an
Apache and advise him: Should they surrender?

———✦———

I N MARCH 1886, GERONIMO AND HIS APACHES HAD SURRENDERED
in Mexico to Gen. George Crook at Cañon de los Embudos. But
they got drunk, and, believing a bootlegger's lies that the soldiers planned to kill them once they crossed the border, Geronimo
and 37 other Apaches stormed back to Mexico's Sierra Madre.

By mid-August, Geronimo knew their odyssey was near-
ing its end. Starvation stalked his people. Mexican troops
dogged their every move, and, if they crossed the border, U.S.
troops sniffed at their heels. Geronimo decided to take his
chances with his old foe, Mexico.

He sent two women, Tahdeste and possibly Lozen, to officials in Fronteras, saying: The Apaches "did not wish to harm
the Mexicans any longer, but wished to secure a peaceful home
with them." In return for peace, they wanted food and mescal.
This they got. The women returned with three laden ponies.

In truth, neither side played fair. Geronimo really wanted
provisions, particularly mescal. The Mexicans, who moved 200
soldiers into Fronteras after the women's visit, hoped to lure
Geronimo's people into Fronteras and slaughter them.

When the women arrived with their precious cargo, the
Apaches "partied" for three days until the mescal ran out.
Geronimo longed for more of the brew. Instead he got visitors.

A fter trying for months with no success to hunt down and
capture the renegade Apaches, Gen. Nelson A. Miles, who
had assumed command of the Department of Arizona from

Crook, had assigned 2nd Lt. Charles B. Gatewood to find Geronimo and convince him to surrender. The Apaches respected Gatewood's integrity. He had been the agent at Fort Apache and had the best chance of catching even a glimpse of the elusive Indians.

Miles assigned Gatewood two peaceful Apaches from Fort Apache that he felt Geronimo might allow into his camp. One, Martine, who was a Nednhi, had trained as a warrior alongside Geronimo's brother-in-law Juh. The other, Kayitah, had a cousin, Yahnozha, who also was Geronimo's brother-in-law and was in the war leader's camp.They agreed to go.

Besides the two scouts, Gatewood's party consisted of interpreter George Wratten, packer Frank Huston, and two pack mules. Later Gatewood hired a courier named Old Tex Whaley at a salary of $100 a month.

On July 19, 1886, the party entered Mexico. On August 3, they hooked up with Capt. Henry W. Lawton, commander of Troop B, 4th Cavalry, about 40 miles southwest of Nacori, Sonora. Lawton had been searching in vain for the Apaches for close to five months and was frustrated— "I'd cry if it would do any good," he wrote his wife, Mame.

Gatewood's arrival did nothing to improve Lawton's mood. Lt. James Parker, who escorted Gatewood into Mexico, wrote, "When told about Gatewood, Lawton objected strongly to taking him with his command."

To Mame, Lawton wrote, "Gatewood is coming out. He wants me to wait and ask Geronimo to surrender. I shall not wait if I find a trail."

However, by the next day he had apparently warmed to the idea as he wrote Mame, "I will do all I can for Gatewood by making it hot for Geronimo."

Gatewood also approached his assignment with little enthusiasm. On the day Gatewood arrived, Dr. Leonard Wood, attached to Lawton's troop as an assistant surgeon, reported, "Gatewood stated that he has no faith in this plan and is disgusted with it. Wants to go home." Gatewood even asked Wood to put him "on sick report, but I do not think his case warrants it." (However, Gatewood did suffer from ill health throughout the campaign.)

The soldiers trudged on. It rained almost every night and temperatures in the sun hovered at 127 degrees, according to Wood's journal.

When word came from Fronteras on August 18 that Geronimo had put out peace feelers to the Mexicans, Lawton ordered Gatewood to head out with his two scouts. Again, the dissension between the Lawton forces and Gatewood surfaced.

Wood wrote, "Late in the evening Lawton came to me full of indignation because Gatewood has not yet left; he had a good mind to put him under his arrest and turn his work over to someone else."

Gatewood headed out at 2 A.M. on August 19 with an escort of six soldiers. His arrival in Fronteras annoyed the Mexican prefect, Jesus Aguirre. After telling Gatewood "to go back where he came from," he "insisted that the Americans should not move in the direction the squaws [carrying the supplies to Geronimo] had taken, because they would interfere with his well laid plans."

In seeming obedience, Gatewood left Fronteras going south, the way he had come. After about 6 miles, he said, he "darted up a convenient arroyo," and swung north where he cut the trail of the women and their heavily laden ponies. Carrying a century plant pole with a white cotton sack tied to it, he pressed forward.

After three days, Kayitah and Martine determined Geronimo's forces "occupied an exceedingly rocky position high up in the Torres [Teras] Mountains." They camped in a canebrake on the Bavispe River about 4 miles from Geronimo's camp with their flag tied high in a century plant. Gatewood sent Martine and Kayitah ahead to make the initial overture to the edgy Apaches. At the same time, he sent Old Tex back to Lawton, suggesting he and his men move forward.

"We realized the danger," the two scouts said in their official report, "but we had promised General Miles that we would try our best to bring back Geronimo and we intended to do it."

Geronimo's nephew, Kanseah, an apprentice warrior about 15 years old, told Eve Ball in *Indeh: An Apache Odyssey*, "I was on guard at the top of the zigzag trail. I lay with field glasses, watching. When I detected a movement on the plain far below, I watched it carefully. Something was coming." He ran to Geronimo, who called his warriors into council. As the specks grew larger, "I recognized Martine and Kayitah by their walk. I could see their faces and told Geronimo who they were."

"It doesn't matter who they are," Geronimo growled. "If they come closer, they are to be shot."

Yahnozha protested, "They are our brothers. Let's find out why they come; they are brave men to risk this."

"They do not take the risk for us, but for the money promised by the White Eyes. When they get close enough, shoot!" Geronimo said.

Yahnozha countered, "We will not shoot. If there is any shooting done, it will be at you, not them. The first man who lifts a rifle I will kill."

"I will help you," Fun said.

Geronimo, "bitter mad" toward the scouts who had led Gatewood to his hideout but realizing he was outnumbered, grunted, "Let them come."

As they got closer, Yahnozha yelled down, "Come on in. Nobody's going to hurt you."

Blunt and to the point, the scout Kayitah told Geronimo:

> The troops are coming after you from all directions. Their aim is to kill everyone of you if it takes 50 years. Everything is against you. If you are awake at night and a rock rolls down the mountain or a stick breaks, you will be running. You even eat your meals running. You have no friends whatever in the world.

Not knowing that Miles intended to send Geronimo's band into exile, Kayitah softened his approach and expounded on the virtues of reservation life.

Grumbling, Geronimo agreed to meet with Gatewood,

LEFT TO RIGHT, PERICO, GERONIMO, NAICHE, AND TSISNAH IN MEXICO FOR THE FIRST 1886 SURRENDER.

whom the Apaches called Bay-chen-daysen, The Beak, because of his prominent nose. Geronimo insisted that Martine stay while Kayitah went back to arrange the conference with Gatewood.

Martine and Kayitah reported:

Geronimo had cooked some mescal [fruit] and from this he took in his two hands enough of this mescal to make a lump about the size of a man's heart. This he squeezed together, wrapped it up and told us to take this to Lt. Gatewood. He said that this was a token of his agreement and that when the mescal had been sent, there would be no reason for Gatewood to doubt his earnestness in planning to make peace.

Knowing that even with this gift Gatewood might be a little nervous about the upcoming meeting, Naiche, whose word was sacred, sent a separate message. He assured the lieutenant of safe-conduct, "so long as we behaved ourselves," Gatewood recalled.

Martine returned to Gatewood's camp just at sundown. Lawton's scouts had arrived, and Lawton followed not far behind. Gatewood said, "Geronimo had sent a message back to say that he would talk with *me* only, & that he was rather offended at our not coming straight to his *rancheria*, where peaceably inclined people were welcome."

Gatewood took Geronimo's gift of mescal and sliced it, then put it between pieces of bread for his soldiers.

At sunrise August 25, Gatewood started for Geronimo's camp with his and Lawton's scouts, but three armed warriors met them and delivered a message from Naiche. The scouts must return to their camp. Gatewood and his small party could meet with him and Geronimo at a bend in the Bavispe River where wood, water, grass, and shade were available.

Reaching this spot, Gatewood and his men unsaddled their mules and set them to grazing.

Before long, the Apaches began arriving, a few at a time, turning their mounts out to graze. Then Geronimo arrived. He put down his Winchester rifle and shook hands with Gatewood.

"He remarked my thinness & apparent bad health & asked what was the matter with me," recalled Gatewood, who had indeed been ill.

Geronimo sat so close to Gatewood that his revolver pressed into the soldier's thigh.

Naiche arrived last. He "was very blue," Gatewood recalled. "All he had to say was that he wanted to meet his children."

Gatewood later wrote that being surrounded by wild Apaches made him feel "chilly twitching movements." Wratten, the interpreter, made the same point: "Well, yes, we did begin to feel a *little* creepy when we saw we were so badly outnumbered and surrounded."

Gatewood passed out tobacco that everyone wrapped Apache-style in oak leaves. He later wrote his wife, Georgia,

"They cracked lots of jokes and smoked lots of tobacco & were in a jolly good humor generally."

Geronimo then asked to hear General Miles' message.

Gatewood took a deep breath.

"Unconditional surrender, and you will be sent to join the rest of your friends in Florida, there to await the decision of the President as to your final disposition. Accept these terms or fight it out to the bitter end."

Then came "a silence of weeks," Gatewood recalled.

Breaking the silence, Geronimo held out his trembling hands and asked for more mescal. He told the lieutenant of the Apaches' three-day drunk, which he stated with evident pride, had occurred "without a single fight."

Learning the soldiers had no liquor, Geronimo resumed negotiations. Since he was getting nowhere with The Beak, he and his warriors "withdrew to one side in the canebrake and held a private conference for an hour or so," Gatewood wrote.

After they broke for lunch, Geronimo took the initiative again and looking Gatewood in the eye, said, "Take us to the reservation or fight."

The color drained from Gatewood's face. "I couldn't take him to the reservation," he wrote later. "I couldn't fight; neither could I run, nor yet feel comfortable."

Naiche, true to his word, reminded Gatewood "that whether they continued the war or not," he and his men "would be allowed to depart in peace," if they behaved and didn't start any violence.

Gatewood relaxed. "Knowing [Naiche's] influence among them, I felt considerably easier in my mind."

Gatewood now played his trump card. Their families were already in Florida, he told them, and only their enemies remained at Fort Apache. (The families had not left Arizona, but Gatewood believed they had.)

This news visibly stunned the Apaches and prompted another hour-long conference in the canebrake. Returning, Geronimo announced they would continue the war, but wanted to kill a beef and continue the conference into the night.

Exhausted, Gatewood had no desire to do so, but agreed. When no cattle could be found, Geronimo suggested they suspend the conference for the night.

He then turned his attention to General Miles. What kind of man was he? He asked about the general's physical characteristics — his age, size, color of hair and eyes, whether his voice was harsh or agreeable to the ears. More importantly he asked about his influence with his own people. Were his words true? Did he have many friends? Did his soldiers and officers like him? Would he keep his promises?

The Apaches hung on Gatewood's every response.

Geronimo summed up the Apaches' analysis of Gatewood's answers. Looking directly at Gatewood, he said, "He must be a good man since the Great Father sent him from Washington, and he sent you all this distance to us."

As night approached, Gatewood prepared to return to Lawton's camp. The Apaches would continue their discussion throughout the night, and Gatewood suggested Geronimo have his medicine man "take a few glances into the future."

One final question from a torn Geronimo shows how much the Apaches respected Gatewood. "We want your advice," Geronimo said to Gatewood. "Consider yourself one of us and not a white man. Remember all that has been said today, and as an Apache, what would you advise us to do under the circumstances?"

"I would trust General Miles and take him at his word." Gatewood responded.

Geronimo, with She-gha by his side, Naiche, and their warriors, sat in council throughout the night. Geronimo voted for continuing on the warpath.

Another warrior suggested killing Gatewood, but Naiche, true to his promise, vetoed any such plan, then sat back, seeming war weary and discouraged. Gatewood's news that the Apaches' relatives were already in Florida weighed heavily on many of the warriors.

Describing the incident as he heard it later from Kanseah, James Kaywaykla said, "The warriors whose families were with them wanted to remain free. It was the lure of being reunited with their wives and children that turned the tide of opinion among the others."

Jason Betzinez heard the story from relatives who were there. In *I Fought with Geronimo*, he wrote that Perico, Geronimo's brother, relented first. "I am going to surrender," he said. "My wife and children have been captured. I love them and want to be with them."

His brother Fun and Ahnandia, another relative and close ally, also voiced their desire to see their families.

Geronimo knew he was outvoted. He stood for a few moments and then said, "I don't know what to do. I have been depending heavily on you three men. You have been great fighters in battle. If you are going to surrender, there is no use my going without you. I will give up with you."

Early the next morning, August 26, the Apaches approached Lawton's camp. Gatewood went out to meet with "our handsome friend." After seating themselves under an ancient mesquite some distance from the camp, Geronimo reported the decision of the council to Gatewood: "If you will give your word that we can meet General Miles with safety, we will go to him and accept his terms."

Then Geronimo relayed the Apaches' terms for surrender. They would not relinquish their weapons until they had formally surrendered to Miles in the United States; Lawton must escort them out of Mexico and protect them from both Mexican and U.S. troops; and Gatewood must travel with them, eating with them and sleeping with them at night.

Gatewood agreed and took him to meet Lawton, which resulted in "a hugging match before the whole command," Gatewood said. All of the Apaches then entered Lawton's camp.

Geronimo told Lawton, "We have not slept for six months and are worn out." Naiche, Wood said, "looked thin, and has not entirely recovered from a wound received several weeks ago in a fight with some American ranchers down near Cumpas." Geronimo ate dinner with the soldiers, "eating heartily of everything," according to Wood.

Gatewood wrote to his wife that the Apaches just wanted to be with their families. He couldn't blame them, he wrote. "Wouldn't I prance around lively if they moved you off to Florida."

G eronimo and his small band of 37 men, women, and children had held off 5,000 U.S. soldiers (about one-quarter of the U.S. Army) and 2,500 Mexican soldiers for months. Now their life of riding like the wind had ended. Another, much less satisfying, waited to begin.

Gatewood, for all his troubles, ran afoul of Miles, who wanted all the glory of the Geronimo surrender. He resented Gatewood, whom he considered Crook's protégé (actually Gatewood and Crook's relationship was contentious). When the citizens of Tucson planned a celebration dinner for Gatewood, Miles ordered him "to stay behind and look after the office [in Los Angeles] during his absence — a clerk's work and unnecessary," Georgia Gatewood wrote of her husband's ignominious treatment.

When people questioned Miles, whom President Theodore Roosevelt later called a "strutting peacock," about Gatewood's absence, he became upset. He was, he said, "sick of this adulation" given to Gatewood, who "only did his duty."

Gatewood spent the rest of his short life in obscurity. He died on May 20, 1896, at the age of 43.

CHAPTER FOURTEEN

The Fourth and Final Surrender

"I will quit the warpath and live at peace,"
Geronimo said. Years later, he said, "I do not
believe that I have ever violated that treaty."

———◦◦◦———

G ENERAL NELSON A. MILES' AMBULANCE ROLLED OUT OF southeastern Arizona's Skeleton Canyon headed back to Fort Bowie. It was September 4, 1886. Geronimo, Naiche, interpreter George Wratten, and three other warriors rode in the back of the carriage.

In the ambulance, the Apache war leader said, "This is the fourth time I have surrendered."

"And I think it is the last time," Miles replied.

Only a week before, starving and exhausted, Geronimo had reached an agreement in Mexico with 2nd Lt. Charles B. Gatewood, who had tracked him and his band to their remote Sierra Madre hideaway with the help of Chiricahua Apache scouts Martine and Kayitah. Geronimo agreed to surrender to Miles at Skeleton Canyon, a time-honored and well-traveled raiding route between Mexico and the United States.

The Apaches and the soldiers set out for Skeleton Canyon on August 26. The always-suspicious Apaches, riding with Gatewood and interpreter George Wratten, traveled some distance away from the military escort commanded by Capt. Henry A. Lawton. "We went along by ourselves," Wratten wrote, "out of sight most of the time of any troops."

The Apaches' foresight in demanding the Army's protection on this journey became evident on the third day: "[W]e saw 600 [actually about 200] Mexicans, soldiers who had come upon us without our noticing their approach," Martine recalled.

Geronimo became nervous, fearing the two armies had plotted to trap him and his people. Gatewood offered to ride with him. They galloped northward and hid. They watched to see how Lawton's command would deal with the Mexican forces.

Army surgeon Leonard Wood rode to meet the Mexicans, explaining that the Apaches had surrendered to the Americans. If the Mexicans came farther, he said, "both the hostile Indians and ourselves were united and in a position to attack them as they came out of the canebrake." (Geronimo had sent word that he was an ally in case of trouble with the Mexicans.)

Mexican commander Jesus Aguirre, the prefect of Arispe, was bitterly disappointed that a longtime adversary had slipped from his grasp. He demanded to meet with Geronimo to be sure that Geronimo indeed planned on surrendering to the U.S. Army.

Geronimo refused to meet Aguirre until Lawton promised protection. Gatewood described the first tense moments:

Geronimo at the head of his party came through the bushes, dragging his Winchester rifle by the muzzle with his left hand, & his six-shooter handy in front of his left hip. The suspicious old rascal would take no chances. As he approached I introduced him to the prefect. After shaking hands, the Mexican shoved his revolver around to his front & Geronimo drew his half way out of the holster, the whites of his eyes turning red, & a most fiendish expression on his face. The former put his hands behind him & the latter dropped his right hand by his side.

An audible sigh passed through the group. When the shaken prefect asked Geronimo why he hadn't surrendered at Fronteras, Geronimo answered that he had not wanted to be murdered.

"Are you going to surrender to the Americans?" Aguirre asked him.

"I am; for I can trust them not to murder me and my people," Geronimo responded.

"Then," Aguirre said, "I shall go along and see that you do surrender."

"No! *You* are going *south* and *I* am going *north*," Geronimo retorted. "I'll have nothing to do with you nor with any of your people."

A soldier writing of this confrontation noted, "I was standing to one side a few feet from the Indians, and what impressed me was the scowls on the Indians' faces and the hatred they showed towards the Mexicans."

Geronimo and Naiche camped close to Lawton's troops that night and then moved out ahead of the Army.

For the next few days the trip went smoothly. Once, Gatewood later recalled, Geronimo's brother Perico, "with considerable grace and dignity," invited Gatewood and other officers to dinner. He described the meal as "a toothsome repast." Prepared by Biyaneta, Perico's wife, it consisted of fresh venison and "flour, sugar, and coffee the thrifty woman had brought with her."

Wood recalled a gracious Naiche saying, "You are in our camp, but our camp is your camp, and you can be here just as at home."

One evening, Geronimo became enamored of Wood's Hotchkiss, a new model of gun. When he asked to see it, Wood reluctantly handed it over with some ammunition. Geronimo fired it, just missing one of his warriors. He howled with laughter as he rolled on the ground, repeating, "Good gun, good gun."

When they arrived at Guadalupe Canyon on the border, "Considerable uneasiness was manifested by the Indians," Gatewood wrote. They had fought here against Lawton's troops sometime before, killing several, and now worried the troopers might seek revenge. Adding to their worries, their protector Lawton had left to speak with Miles.

Geronimo had good reason to be concerned. Lawton's

second-in-command, Lt. Abiel Smith, "expressed a desire to pitch in with the troop & have it out right there."

When Geronimo learned of this, the Apaches jumped on their ponies, and with the women and children at the front, dashed out of the canyon. Gatewood chased after and rode beside Geronimo, as the military escort followed at a distance.

Geronimo asked Gatewood what he would do if the soldiers started firing. The lieutenant replied that he would try to stop them, but if that didn't work, "I will run away with you."

Naiche said, "You must go with us, for fear some of our men might believe you treacherous and try to kill you."

Gatewood returned to talk to Smith. When Smith insisted on "talking" to Geronimo and the Apaches, Gatewood "threatened to blow the head off the first man if he didn't stop."

Meanwhile, Miles stalled, certain his superiors would hold him accountable, as they had Crook, if the Apaches broke away. He urged Lawton to accept the Apaches' surrender himself.

By August 30, Gatewood, Lawton, who had rushed back to his camp upon hearing of the plot on the Apaches' lives, and the Apaches had arrived at San Bernardino, Arizona.

Lawton feared the Apaches would bolt. He wrote his wife, "I am too anxious and worried to write you much. I cannot get the General to come out and see them and they are very uneasy about it." And he sent a message to Miles, stating:

> I have no idea hostiles will surrender to me or anyone but the General. To deliver up their arms and surrender unconditionally, they, it appears, believe means that some of them will be killed. They prefer to die with arms in their hands and fighting. It is difficult task to surprise and surround them when they are watching your every movement.

Geronimo, too, tired of waiting for the foot-dragging general. "I sent my brother Porico [sic] with Mr. George Wratten on to Fort Bowie to see General Miles, and to tell him that we wished to return to Arizona," he said.

Still Miles refused to come, and his messages became ever more aggressive, telling Lawton, "You can use any other means you think available. You will be justified in using any measure," implying that murder would be looked upon favorably.

Lawton replied that the Indians "were alert and watchful, and to surprise them is simply impossible. I could by treachery perhaps kill one or two of them, but it would only make everything much worse than before."

Finally, on September 2, Miles left for Skeleton Canyon. Still trying to shield himself from political failure, he sent word to Gen. Oliver O. Howard, commander of the Division of the Pacific, that he did not "anticipate any favorable result. They are still in the mountains and not within the control of our forces."

Lawton, Gatewood, and the Apaches moved to Skeleton Canyon on that same day. They found troops already there. This spooked the Apaches, who showed signs of flight. With Gatewood trailing along, Geronimo moved his camp about 2 miles away to a defensible place in the mountains. Naiche moved even higher.

On September 3, Geronimo and Gatewood watched the activity below them, waiting for something to happen. Miles arrived at 3 P.M., and Geronimo rode in with Gatewood from the Apaches' mountain camp. He dismounted, leaving his weapons on his horse, shook hands with Miles, "and then stood proudly before the officers."

"General Miles is your friend," an interpreter said.

"I never saw him," Geronimo replied, "but I have been in need of friends. Why has he not been with me?"

Nervous laughter broke out as the interpreter translated these words, breaking the tension. Geronimo glanced around, seeming surprised by the laughter, then grinned and turned back to Miles. He related his grievances, telling Miles how Mickey Free and Chatto, two of the Army's Apache scouts, had conspired against him, causing him to jump the reservation.

Although not easily awed, Miles was impressed by his wild adversary. He later wrote:

He was one of the brightest, most resolute, determined looking men that I have ever encountered. He had the clearest, sharpest, dark eyes I think I have ever seen, unless it was that of General Sherman when he was at the prime of life. Every movement indicated power, energy and determination.

He outlined the terms of surrender to Geronimo. Playing to the Apaches' biggest concern, he said "Lay down your arms and come with me to Fort Bowie, and in five days you will see your families now in Florida with [Chief] Chihuahua, and no harm will be done you."

When Geronimo asked to return to the reservation in Arizona's White Mountains, Miles lied and told him he had sent all the Apaches out of the West. This "seemed to dishearten him more than any other fact of the situation," Miles recalled.

Miles then drew a line in the dirt. "This represents the ocean," he said. Putting a small stone beside the line, he continued, "This represents the place where Chihuahua is with his band." Placing another stone some distance away, he said, "This represents you, Geronimo." He placed a third stone close to the second. "This represents the Indians at Camp Apache." Picking up the second and third stones, he placed them with the first, representing Chief Chihuahua. "That is what the President wants to do, get all of you together."

Geronimo turned to Gatewood and smiled. In Apache, he said, "Good, you told the truth."

Now convinced that Miles was his friend, Geronimo followed him everywhere, "as if fearing he might go away, leaving his captive behind."

After moving to the Army camp on September 4, Geronimo asked Gatewood to go with him to find Naiche, who had stayed in the hills with the rest of the small band. Supposedly, a relative who'd gone back to Mexico looking for a favorite pony had not returned. Believing him dead, Naiche now mourned for him.

They found Naiche on a ridge, staring toward Mexico.

ARMY SCOUT MICKEY FREE GREW UP AMONG THE APACHES
AFTER BEING CAPTURED AS A CHILD.

Gatewood informed him that not greeting the white chief was discourteous. Naiche agreed. He came in that afternoon. Miles presented the terms of surrender to him as the chief. He accepted them as well.

Miles indicated that he did not quite buy the "lost relative" excuse. He said, "Naiche was wild and suspicious and evidently feared treachery. The last hereditary chief of the hostile Apaches hesitated to place himself in the hands of the palefaces."

Knowing the importance of ceremony to the Apaches, Miles made the surrender ceremony as impressive as possible under the circumstances. In his memoirs, Geronimo recalled:

We stood between his troopers and my warriors. We placed a large stone on the blanket before us. Our treaty was made by this stone, and it was to last till the stone should crumble to dust; so we made the treaty, and bound each other with an oath. We raised our hands to heaven and took an oath not to do any wrong to each other or to scheme against each other.

Then Geronimo said to Miles, "I will quit the warpath and live at peace hereafter." It was done.

Geronimo later said, "I did not greatly believe General Miles, but because the President of the United States had sent me word, I agreed to make the treaty, and keep it. I do not believe that I have ever violated that treaty."

By the next morning, all of the Apaches had entered the military encampment. At 10 A.M., with Geronimo, Naiche, and the three other Apaches loaded in his ambulance, Miles began the 65-mile journey to Fort Bowie. He told the driver, "Don't let the sun go down on you," showing his sense of urgency. The Apaches rode in the back of the ambulance, still fully armed, and Miles sat in front with the driver. Lt. Thomas Clay rode behind the conveyance with orders, he said, to "kill anyone who attempted to escape."

When they reached the fort, Geronimo and the other Apaches gave up their arms. Miles found a telegram from Howard, stating, "The surrender of Geronimo and his Apaches is reported in the evening papers. Report the same officially."

Knowing that, if word got out that the Apaches were at Fort Bowie, he might not be able to protect them, Miles waited until the following day to wire his superiors:

The Indians surrendered as prisoners of war on sept fourth. I returned here last night bringing Geronimo Natchez [sic] hereditary Chief and three others. Lawton will bring in the remainder tomorrow about 40 in all —

**NOW PRISONERS OF WAR, APACHES
FROM GERONIMO'S BAND HUDDLE AT FORT BOWIE.**

Indians are perfectly submissive and will do whatever I
say—I intend to ship them to Florida in a few days unless otherwise ordered—Geronimo says reason he broke
out was that Chatto and micke free [sic] had laid plot to
kill him. That statement is Confirmed by others and not
disproved by [Mickey Free's] face.

    The country howled for the Apaches' extermination. The
Tucson Daily Citizen suggested a "peace—that peace that pas-
seth all understanding." The *New York Times* reported that it
was a comfort to think the Apaches might die of yellow fever
in Florida.

    Unaware of the danger they might be in, Geronimo, Naiche,
and the other three Apaches seemed content and relaxed now
that they were no longer, in their minds at least, enemies of
the whites. They wandered around the fort as they waited for
Lawton to bring in the rest of their people. They shopped at
the trader's store, buying boots and other items with silver
coins stolen from the Mexicans.

While waiting, Miles kept up his propaganda. He promised to wipe out the Apaches' past sins as if they'd never happened and urged them to "Leave your horses here, maybe they will be sent to you. You will have a separate reservation with your tribe, with horses and wagons, and no one will harm you."

Geronimo remembered Miles promising: "I will build you a house; I will fence you much land; I will give you cattle, horses, mules, and farming implements. . . . There is plenty of timber, water, and grass in the land to which I will send you. You will live with your tribe and with your family."

Almost two decades later, Geronimo said, "I looked in vain for General Miles to send me to that land of which he had spoken."

Miles, for all his self-serving ways and the lies he told the Apaches, now determined to see them safely out of Arizona Territory. He cordoned off the post from civilian authorities, whose dearest wish was to hang Geronimo and his band from the nearest cottonwood tree. President Grover Cleveland expressed the same feelings, saying, "I hope nothing will be done with Geronimo which will prevent our treating him as a prisoner of war, if we cannot hang him, which I would much prefer."

The rest of the Apaches, under Lawton, Gatewood, and Wood arrived the morning of September 8. On the trip in, Geronimo had become a grandfather again. Nocton, the wife of his son Chappo, had given birth to a daughter.

Wood said, "The command halted perhaps an hour for this purpose and then took up the march, the girl carrying her young baby. She looked pretty pale, but otherwise seemed to pay little attention to the incident." Other reports said she climbed back on her horse and rode the rest of the way while Chappo carried the infant.

As soon as they arrived, Miles placed all the Apaches in wagons. As the wagons rolled through the cactus-studded hills of Apache Pass under the heavy guard of the 4th Cavalry, the military band on the parade ground broke into *Auld Lang Syne*. While the soldiers laughed, the Indians stared at them curiously.

**NAICHE AND GERONIMO IN FRONT OF
FORT BOWIE'S CAVALRY BARRACKS, JUST BEFORE
LEAVING FOR THE TRAIN TO FLORIDA.**

On the way to Bowie Station, acting Assistant Adjutant General William A. Thompson, his tongue loosened by a few drinks, patted his pocket and confided in Wood that he had something that would stop the entire parade. "But," Thompson said, "I am not going to let the old man see it until you are gone, then I will repeat it to him."

In his pocket were orders from Washington, D.C. to hold the Indians in Arizona for trial by a civil court.

The train left Bowie Station at 2:55 P.M. Geronimo and his band had touched Arizona soil for the last time. Their journey to Florida and 27 years as prisoners of war had begun. Lawton, Wood, and Wratten accompanied them, along with two officers and 20 men of the 4th Cavalry. Miles went as far as the New Mexico border, to see them safely out of his jurisdiction.

Miles had promised Martine and Kayitah, the scouts who helped Gatewood find Geronimo, $3,000 and good homes at Fort Apache if Geronimo surrendered. Incredibly, soldiers grabbed them at the last minute and loaded them onto the train as prisoners of war. They never received anything Miles promised them, except small pensions 40 years later.

The other scouts received the same treatment, although many had never fought against the whites. General Crook's aide John G. Bourke wrote, "There is no more disgraceful page in the history of our relations with the American Indians than that which conceals the treachery visited upon the Chiricahuas who remained faithful in their allegiance to our people."

Their betrayal, however, pleased many Apaches. Geronimo's nephew Asa Daklugie told author Eve Ball, "There was just one good thing in the whole procedure; the scouts who had betrayed their people were doomed to captivity like the rest of us. The loyal Apaches made it miserable for the cowardly traitors."

Miles and Lawton took no small credit for the surrender and ultimate confinement of Geronimo and the Apaches. Miles wrote to his wife, "If you had been here, you would have seen me riding in over the mountains with Geronimo and Naiche. It was a brilliant ending to a difficult problem." The general took Geronimo's rifle and spurs as personal souvenirs.

GERONIMO!

The Prisoner of War

**THE OLD WAR LEADER AS
HE LOOKED A FEW YEARS
BEFORE DYING IN 1909.**

Stopped in San Antonio

*As prisoners of war, Geronimo, Naiche, and their
band set off by train for their Florida exile,
a sorrowful trip that almost dead-ended in Texas.*

———❖———

O FFICIALS IN THE WAR DEPARTMENT WERE ANGERED WHEN
they realized that Miles had spirited the Apaches out of
Arizona. Why, they asked, had he disobeyed a direct
order to hold the Apaches?

He had already shipped them out before he got the wire,
he answered. This was true. William A. Thompson, acting
Assistant Adjutant General, had held the telegram until the
Apaches were well on their way.

Nevertheless, why was Miles in such a hurry to ship
them out? Because, he said, they had ordered him to place
them "beyond the reach of escape."

On September 10, 1886, the War Department ordered Brig.
Gen. D.S. Stanley, commander of the Department of Texas, to halt
the train in San Antonio and hold the prisoners until the government decided whether to send the Apaches back to Arizona
and their fate at the hands of the civil authorities or to send
them on to Florida.

A local newspaper described the "hard-looking company"
on their arrival: "Their haggard features and uneasy glances
would have excited pity in the hearts of anyone who did not
know them."

By September 29, Miles suffered under an even more intense barrage of questions. Officials in Washington had discovered some startling details concerning the Apaches' "capture,"
although it's hard to understand why they thought the Apaches

had been captured: Miles had stated they had surrendered. He simply neglected to say it was a conditional surrender.

The Secretary of War sent an incredulous telegram to Miles:

It would appear that Geronimo, instead of being captured, surrendered, and that the surrender, instead of being unconditional, was, contrary to expectations here, accompanied with conditions and promises.

Meanwhile, Geronimo and his fellow Apaches stayed in San Antonio, living in tents set up in the quadrangle at Fort Sam Houston and fearing for their lives. Geronimo's nephew Kanseah told Eve Ball, "When they put us on that train at Bowie, nobody thought that we'd get far before they'd stop it and kill us." Photographs of Geronimo taken then show the deep strain he was under.

George Wratten, their white interpreter, also feared for their safety. Geronimo spoke with him about his warriors. "It is for them that I fear," the war leader said. "They are unarmed. If we had weapons, we would fight it out as we have in the past." He felt no concern for himself. His Power had long ago promised he would die a natural death.

Wratten deliberated long and hard, then told Geronimo he had guns and ammunition in his tent. If attacked, the warriors should get them. "I can't let unarmed men be murdered even if I have to join them," he told Geronimo.

Even with these assurances, the Apaches knew the odds were stacked against them. Kanseah recalled that his mother told him, "that if an attack came I was to show these White Eyes how an Apache can die."

While they feared for their lives, their distance from Arizona Territory guaranteed the Apaches celebrity status. People swarmed to see the "Tigers of the Desert," as Gen. George Crook had referred to Geronimo and his warriors.

The San Antonio press reported widely on their stay. One reporter described Geronimo as "5 foot 8 inches in height and

EN ROUTE TO SAN ANTONIO. FRONT ROW, LEFT TO RIGHT, ARE FUN, PERICO, NAICHE, GERONIMO, CHAPPO, AND AN APACHE BOY. LOZEN IS THIRD FROM RIGHT IN THE BACK ROW.

9,000 feet in meanness." Another wrote, "The bloodthirsty villains are gazed at, covered with given flowers and delicacies, as if they were heroes."

Still another said, "They have been taken around in carriages to see the sights and have even been conducted into the Lone Star Brewery there." While at the brewery, Geronimo tried to taste the local brew, but the officials held him back, while Naiche, after inspecting a piece of ice he had been given, put it in his pocket. The article went on to complain that the townsfolk barely noticed Lawton and his men, while Geronimo was "the recipient of bouquets, the children supplied with candy, and the squaws with ribbons, money, etc., by the best ladies of the city."

On September 15, the *Atlanta Constitution* reported 10,000 people had visited the prisoners that day, then added, "They cannot be seen tomorrow as they and the troops require some

**GERONIMO TENSELY WAITING
AT FORT SAM HOUSTON.**

rest." The report went on to describe Geronimo's "amusing" contortions after "gorging himself with fresh beef" and 50-cents worth of candy.

While on display, Geronimo decked himself out in all his sartorial splendor. Wearing a gray alpaca jacket — a favorite garment — a white straw hat, and white trousers, which he wore tucked inside his new Army boots, he cut a dashing, if somewhat incongruous figure — over the pants he wore the requisite breechclout.

As usual, rumors sprang up around him. One that still endures concerns the tower in the fort's quadrangle. Some soldiers took Geronimo to the top to see the countryside. While he stood on the balcony 60 feet up, so the story goes, the bell in the clock struck the hour, so frightening him that he jumped off. As he would have hit the ground in 1.9 seconds with a fatal force of 9,610 foot pounds, this is obviously untrue. The truth is that Geronimo feared the soldiers would push him off the balcony and refused to step out upon it.

While the investigation trying to determine what had been promised the Apaches continued into October, they lolled about the quadrangle, played cards, and smoked. Stanley interviewed Geronimo and Naiche separately; each gave a consistent story. They had been promised they would spend two years in Florida on a reservation with green grass and trees with equipment, and people to work the land for them. Most importantly, they would be reunited with their families.

On October 19, Secretary of War William C. Endicott issued President Cleveland's orders. The men, "guilty of the worst crimes known to the law, committed under circumstances of great atrocity," were to be sent "under proper guard to Fort Pickens, Florida, there to be kept in close custody until further orders." The women, children, and the two scouts, Martine and Kayitah, were bound for "Fort Marion, Florida, and placed with the other Apache Indians recently conveyed to and now under custody at that post."

When Geronimo and Naiche heard this pronouncement, they protested bitterly. Their overriding reason for surrendering had been the promise they would be reunited with their families. Stanley sent their statement to Sheridan and the War Department, stating that he believed they were telling the truth. The War Department returned it stamped "Disapproved."

On October 22 at 4 A.M. Stanley ushered his reluctant visitors onto the train. They loaded the men into one car and the women, children and the two scouts into another. A car in between carried enlisted men. The Apache men would not see their families again for eight months.

While Miles had spared their lives, they were now headed for 27 years as prisoners of war and a place that would cause them much heartache and death.

Captive Geronimo Becomes a Profitable Commodity

After Florida cities fought to use him
as a tourist attraction and sideshow, the wily
old raider learned to make a profit on his own.

———※◆※———

T HE NEWS OF GERONIMO'S SURRENDER IN SEPTEMBER 1886 flashed across the nation. The Apache terror had ended. But for the utterly defeated Apaches, the humiliation and exploitation had just begun. Taken from their desert home, they were incarcerated in the high humidity of the Southeast.

"No Apache was ever cruel enough to imprison anyone," Geronimo's nephew Asa Daklugie said. "Only a White Eyes was capable of that."

While the Southwest screamed for Apache blood, the East welcomed the exiles with open arms. Dollar signs, visions of swarming tourists, and the resultant economic boost beckoned. Hoping to influence the War Department's choice of destinations, Florida cities started campaigning for the Apache assignment in a war of words. With close to 500 Apaches already crammed into tiny Fort Marion at St. Augustine (three shipments of Apaches had arrived earlier), Pensacolians started a petition to support jailing the latest band at Fort Pickens on Santa Rosa Island out in Pensacola Bay.

"The painted demons," the petitioners said, would be a "better card than a circus or sea serpent," and give "Pensacola an attraction which will bring her many visitors."

The *Florida Times-Union*, speaking for St. Augustine, rebutted, "Geronimo is the man we want here."

Pensacola prevailed. Geronimo, Naiche, and their warriors would be sent there, while the women, children, and the two scouts who tracked down Geronimo's band, Martine and Kayitah, would be sent to Fort Marion in St. Augustine. *The Pensacolian* proudly stated, "The government has selected the most suitable place to incarcerate the greatest living American general and his principle officers. We welcome the nation's distinguished guests."

When the train arrived in Pensacola, the steamboat *Twin* pulled along side. The soldiers loaded the warriors onto the steamer while the Apache women and children wailed. A crowd had gathered to watch the newest sideshow. As the steamer prepared to chug across the bay, Naiche appeared "much amused," while others watched the dolphins that swam about the boat. Another, probably Ahnandia, who spoke a little English, said mournfully, "Won't see Mexico no more."

Excursion boats left Pensacola daily to see the Apache prisoners. Tourists intruded into every facet of their lives. It was one-stop shopping at its best. "You can go over to Santa Rosa Island, see Fort Pickens and Geronimo, and gather beautiful shells and marine curiosities on the beach," stated the *Pensacola Commercial*. On a record day, 457 Pensacolians made the trip.

The same paper, reporting on Geronimo, said, "He'd exhibit himself to the anxious memento seekers, ostentatiously take off the article and hand it to the purchaser," and conversely, "He is a great beggar and will ask for anything that strikes his fancy."

Another reporter chided regular female visitors. "The ladies who visit these savages indulge in too much gush." One breathless young thing asked a soldier, "Can you tell me what is best for me to give to Geronimo?" He answered, "An ounce of lead between the eyes." This feminine attention didn't go unnoticed by the much-married Geronimo. An observer noted,

"Geronimo recalls the names of several ladies who have paid more than one visit."

The attention paid the prisoners rankled some of the public. A cartoon captioned, "Tired of Murder — Siesta in Florida," ran in *Frank Leslie's Illustrated Newspaper*. In it Geronimo lounges in a hammock smoking a cigar, liquor bottle at hand, while being fanned by Uncle Sam. The Pensacolian stated, "Geronimo and his band got fat in Florida and were well pleased with their 'punishment.'"

Contrary to this supposed life of leisure and luxury, the Apaches suffered both mentally and physically. They were homesick for Arizona and felt certain a death sentence dangled dangerously close over their heads. However Capt. Loomis L. Langdon, the officer in charge of the prisoners at Fort Pickens, reported, "There has been no occasion to reprimand, much less to punish, a single one of these Indians since their arrival here."

They missed their families. Geronimo said, "They put me to sawing up large logs. There were several other Apache warriors with me, and all of us had to work every day. We were kept at hard labor in this place and we did not see our families until May [actually late April] 1887."

In April the Fort Pickens prisoners were joined by those of their families that wished to reunite with them. Geronimo's three wives and their children, and Naiche's three wives and their children, were in the group that went to Fort Pickens. The government sent the remaining Apaches, decimated by malaria and tuberculosis, on to what they considered a healthier climate — Mount Vernon, Alabama.

A little more than a year later, on May 13, 1888, the government also moved Geronimo and his small band from Fort Pickens to Mount Vernon.

Their exotic new residents delighted Alabamians. "The placing of the Indians at Mount Vernon will add greatly to the attractiveness of that place as a Sunday school picnic resort," reported *The Mobile Register*, while railroad officials proclaimed, "Mount Vernon will become a favorite summer resort."

Excursions from as far away as New Orleans visited Apache Village. The docility and friendliness of the Apaches disappointed many. That Geronimo taught Sunday school, kept discipline in the schoolroom, and acted as justice of the peace, earning about $10 a month, seemed incongruous. (His tenure as justice of the peace began with heavy inappropriate punishments. In one case, he sentenced an Apache to 100 years in jail for drunkenness. With training, however, he learned to mete out fair punishments.)

After observing Geronimo, the *Northwestern Lumberman* said, "He was about as mild mannered a man as ever scuttled a ship or cut a throat and for that matter butchered defenseless women and children."

The Apaches' health did not improve at Mount Vernon, and in 1894 the government moved them permanently to Fort Sill, Indian Territory, Oklahoma. Disease had taken its toll. Fewer than 300 Apaches remained, many of them children born into captivity. Almost half of those sent to Florida in 1886 had died.

While the Kiowas and Comanches reconciled themselves to the Apaches living on their land, the white community did not. An observer noted, "Yes, here we go to see the king of murderers and prince of fiery destruction now made glorious by the sentimental adulation of insane freaks and misguided philanthropists. The old devil Geronimo should have been hung 15 years ago."

The post commander, Capt. H.L. Scott, did not like Geronimo, whom he called, "an unlovely character, a crossgrained, mean, selfish old curmudgeon, of whom I never heard recounted a kindly or generous deed." Others disagreed, saying the old warrior was a kindly old man who was generous with his family and others of his tribe.

The soldiers at Fort Sill began calling Geronimo "Gerry," which he hated. Even though they belittled him, and the intense curiosity about him had lessened, one thing remained

FROM LEFT TO RIGHT: GERONIMO, NAICHE, AND MANGUS AT FORT PICKENS IN 1887.

constant. Geronimo was a saleable commodity. He made many personal appearances including the Trans-Mississippi Exposition in Omaha, and the Louisiana Purchase Exposition in St. Louis. He also traveled to wild west shows, including an appearance at the 101 Ranch in Oklahoma. Daklugie said that whenever Geronimo traveled, he would start with a dollar in his pocket. "When we returned, Geronimo would have a supply of good clothes and plenty of money."

Always an innovator, Geronimo was his own best PR man and an astute businessman. He quickly learned that his possessions were in demand. His bows and arrows and anything else he made sold faster and for more money. When he exhausted his supply, he gathered up items belonging to his warriors. Daklugie rationalized, "He didn't tell anybody he made them — people just assumed he did."

Interpreter George Wratten had taught Geronimo to carve walking sticks. After carving his printed "Geronimo" into the wood, he'd charge souvenir seekers $1. When asked why so much, he replied, "Put name, is worth dollar."

This fame, along with a proclivity for making a buck, ensured Geronimo's pockets always jingled. He sold anything anyone wanted to buy. His photo and autograph were always for sale. He once sold a ragged hawk feather plucked from the

**APACHES, MOSTLY WOMEN AND CHILDREN,
AT MOUNT VERNON BARRACKS, ALABAMA, CIRCA 1888.**

ground for $5. On trips, he'd cut the buttons from his coat and sell them for 25 cents each; his hat went for $5. He'd then sew on new buttons and don a new hat (he'd brought along extras), and eagerly await the next stop.

His grandest moment, however, was his trip to the Louisiana Purchase Exposition, where he lived for several months in Apache Village. Several of his old cronies, as well as his grandson, Thomas Dahkeya, and his daughter, Lenna, accompanied him. The magic acts and people from other countries that populated the fair fascinated him. When he laughed uproariously at a puppet show, with what he called "strange little people," he said all the people near him "seemed to be laughing at me." He rode in a "little house that had four windows" and went up in the air—a Ferris wheel.

And he made money. "I often made as much as two dollars a day, and when I returned I had plenty of money—more than I had ever owned before," he said. He may have been too modest—at this time people paid him $2 for an autographed picture and $10 for an autographed bow. Others claimed he made upwards of $50 a day. An observer noted, "The old gentleman is pretty high priced, but then he is the only Geronimo." When Geronimo died, he had more than $10,000 in his bank account.

He came close to stealing President Theodore Roosevelt's thunder when he rode in the new president's 1905 inaugural parade. Heading a delegation of Indian leaders, Geronimo rode in full face paint, head held high, his creased face stoic. According to Daklugie, he wore only a breechcloth, moccasins and his medicine hat — a leather cap with eagle plumes streaming below his stirrups. However, pictures show him wrapped in a blanket, since it was a bitingly cold day.

Woodworth Clum, a newspaperman and the son of John Clum, the only man to ever capture Geronimo, stood near Roosevelt while he reviewed the parade in front of the White House. He asked, "Why did you select Geronimo to march in your own parade, Mr. President? He is the greatest single-handed murderer in American history." Roosevelt replied, "I wanted to give the people a good show."

Daklugie, who usually accompanied Geronimo as his lieutenant, said of the parade, "The cheers for Roosevelt evaporated. Men threw their hats into the air and shouted, 'Hooray for Geronimo!' We were told later that Roosevelt said he never wished to hear the name of Geronimo again."

On this same trip, Wratten and Dr. S.M. Huddleson of the Department of Agriculture took the old Apache to Arlington Cemetery to visit the graves of the soldiers he'd fought against. The bas-relief on Gen. George Crook's monument, which depicted the March 1886 surrender scene at Cañon de los Embudos, fascinated him. At the grave of Charles B. Gatewood, the man who had convinced him to surrender, "We shook hands all around in" Gatewood's memory, recalled Huddleson.

The years passed and the Apaches remained in captivity, but people still worried they would break out and wreak havoc. At the Omaha Exposition, Geronimo and Naiche, along with several of their friends, rented a wagon almost every weekend to see the countryside. On one such trip, Jimmie Stevens, whose pony Geronimo had killed many years before, accompanied

**GERONIMO, IN TOP HAT, AND OTHER INDIANS
POSE ON AN OKLAHOMA RANCH IN 1905.**

them. As they started back, according to Stevens, after "visiting several ranches" and eating "many melons and squash," they got lost. Darkness fell. It was cloudy so they had no stars or moon to guide them. And, as Geronimo put it, "No mountains. Nothing but corn in this damn country." They wandered for several hours before finding their way home.

"When he didn't come in at dark," said Stevens, "they thought he and Naiche had pulled out and gone." The excitable public sent out an alarm. The headlines of the extra read "Geronimo and Nachee [sic] escape. Apache murderers thought to be on their way back to Arizona." But, said Stevens, "Geronimo was only lost in the corn."

As Geronimo grew older, interest in him never wavered. For the rest of his life, the Tiger of the Desert would be a huge draw wherever he went.

CHAPTER SEVENTEEN

Longing for Arizona

"Great Father, my hands are tied as with a rope.
I pray you to cut the ropes and make me free.
Let me die in my own country,
an old man who has been punished enough."

— *Geronimo to President Theodore Roosevelt.*

⬥

D URING THE APACHES' LONG IMPRISONMENT, GERONIMO'S dearest wish was to return to Arizona, and he took every opportunity to plead his case.

In 1898 at the Trans-Mississippi and International Exposition in Omaha, he came face to face with Gen. Nelson A. Miles, to whom he had surrendered, a set-up by the promoters of the exposition and of Miles. Asa Daklugie, Geronimo's nephew, described the meeting: "They exchanged some bitter words and each taunted the other with being a liar. Miles smiled and freely admitted that he had lied, and then stated, 'You lied to Mexicans, Americans, and to your own Apaches for 30 years. White men only lied to you once, and I did it.' "

Showing uncommon restraint, Geronimo did not answer Miles' accusation, but instead made a plea to return to Arizona. "The acorns and piñon nuts, and quail and the wild turkey, the giant cactus and the paloverdes — they all miss me. I miss them, too. I want to go back to them."

Miles laughed, ridiculing him, and retorted:

A very beautiful thought, Geronimo. Quite poetic. But the men and women who live in Arizona, they do not miss you. They do not wonder where you have gone; they know. They do not want you to come back. Folks in

Arizona sleep now at night, have no fear that Geronimo
will come and kill them. The acorns and piñon nuts, the
quail and the wild turkey, the giant cactus and the
paloverde trees — they will have to get along as best
they can — without you.

Some newspaper reports say this meeting was even more
acrimonious, that Geronimo saw Miles in the stands, leapt at
him, and tried to murder him. Miles just laughed and said
Geronimo wanted to shake his hand.

Although Miles dismissed his plea, Geronimo got the opportunity to take his case to a higher court. Four days after he
rode in Theodore Roosevelt's 1905 inaugural parade, he and
the other Indian leaders visited the President in the White
House. When presented to Roosevelt, he said:

Great Father, I look to you as I look to God. When
I see your face I think I see the face of the Great Spirit.
I come here to pray you to be good to me and my people.

Did I fear the Great White Chief? No. He was my
enemy and the enemy of my people. His people desired
the country of my people. My heart was strong against
him. I said that he should never have my country. I defied
the Great White Chief, for in those days I was a fool

I ask you to think of me as I was then. I lived in the
home of my people. They trusted me. It was right that I
should give them my strength and my wisdom.

When the soldiers of the Great White Chief drove
me and my people from our home we went to the mountains. When they followed us we slew all that we could.
We said we would not be captured. No. We starved but we
killed. I said that we would never yield, but I was a fool.

So I was punished, and all my people were punished with me. The white soldiers took me and made
me a prisoner far from my own country.

Great Father, other Indians have homes where

**GERONIMO IN CEREMONIAL GARB
AT FORT SILL.**

they can live and be happy. I and my people have no
homes. The place where we are kept is bad for us. We
are sick there and we die. White men are in the country
that was my home. I pray you to tell them to go away and
let my people go there and be happy.

Great Father, my hands are tied as with a rope. My
heart is no longer bad. I will tell my people to obey no
chief but the Great White Chief. I pray you to cut the
ropes and make me free. Let me die in my own country,
an old man who has been punished enough and is free.

Moved by his eloquence, Roosevelt spoke gently, but hon-
estly. "I have no anger in my heart against you." But, he could-
n't let the Apaches return to Arizona, he explained. Enmity
toward them ran high there, even after all these years, and, "I
should have to interfere between you," he said. "There would be
more war and more bloodshed."

In this Roosevelt was correct. Arizona pioneer Edward
Wilson, writing of Arizona's early days, said, "Had Geronimo
been allowed to return, his days would surely have had a most
sudden ending. Many old timers here had had their loved ones

GERONIMO NARRATES HIS MEMOIRS TO S.M. BARRETT (LEFT), WITH ASA DAKLUGIE (RIGHT) TRANSLATING.

killed by Geronimo and his savages — and they had not forgotten."

Roosevelt did agree to take up Geronimo's request with the commissioner of Indian affairs and the secretary of war, "but I do not think I can hold out any hope for you," he said. It's doubtful whether the president actually presented Geronimo's case. No decision was ever rendered.

This did not silence Geronimo. In the last chapter of his autobiography published in 1906, he first thanked President Roosevelt for giving him permission to tell his story. He added, "I hope that he and those in authority under him will read my story and judge whether my people have been rightly treated."

He asked to return to Arizona, stating that Oklahoma had proved unhealthy for the Apaches. He spoke of Arizona's rich soil, the minerals, lush grasses, and forestland they would live on and farm. "We do not ask all of the land which the Almighty gave us in the beginning, but that we may have sufficient lands there to cultivate." In a concession, he said, "What we do not need, we are glad for the white men to cultivate."

And finally, he issued a plea:

I want to spend my last days there, and be buried among those mountains. If this could be, I might die in peace, feeling that my people, placed in their native homes, would increase in numbers, rather than diminish as at present, and that our name would not become extinct. Could I but see this accomplished, I think I could forget all the wrongs that I have ever received, and die a contented and happy old man.

In April 1907 he had his photo taken in Lawton, Oklahoma. According to newspaper reports, he said, "Me want good picture to send to my good friend, President Roosevelt. Maybe so sometime President say, 'Go, good old Geronimo; you killed heap white folks, but Jesus man made you good; be good man all time and war men hold you no more.' "

And in October of that same year, he passed through Oklahoma City. Having heard that the local newspaper had installed a new press, Geronimo insisted on seeing it. He told a reporter, "In the paper, write a letter to the Great White Father in Washington. Say to him: 'Geronimo got religion now. Geronimo fight no more. The old times, he forget. Geronimo want to be prisoner of war no more. He want to be free.' Tell the Great White Father that. Tell him in the paper."

Neither he nor any of his people ever returned to their Arizona homeland. Geronimo died at Fort Sill in Oklahoma, still a prisoner of war.

CHAPTER EIGHTEEN

At the End, Religion

Geronimo's last battle was
a deeply personal one
that lasted to his deathbed.

————◆◆————

THROUGHOUT HIS CAPTIVITY, RELIGION BEDEVILED GERONIMO. Raised in the Apache lifeway, he found it difficult to convert to Christianity, a religion that did not fulfill his needs and that he considered too strict. He found the Apache religion simple and uncomplicated:

We had no churches, no religious organizations, no sabbath day, no holidays, and yet we worshiped. Sometimes the whole tribe would assemble to sing and pray; sometimes a small number, perhaps only two or three. Sometimes we prayed in silence; sometimes each one prayed aloud; sometimes an aged person prayed for all of us. At other times one would rise and speak to us of our duties to each other and to Ussen. Our services were short.

In 1895, Frank Hall Wright, a Choctaw and a minister of the Reformed Church in America, arrived at Fort Sill, Oklahoma, to minister to the Apaches. The church decided to start with a school for the children.

Geronimo responded, "I, Geronimo, and these others are now too old to travel your Jesus road. But our children are young and I and my brothers will be glad to have the children taught about the white man's God."

Soon they began using the school as a church, and while the older Apaches initially shied away from Christianity, first one and then another converted. Naiche became so fervent a believer that he took the name of Christian Naiche. He urged Geronimo to become a Christian. Geronimo was reluctant, but he felt his influence with his people slipping.

During the summer of 1902, Geronimo's wife Zi-yeh attended the yearly camp meeting alone. On the last day, Geronimo appeared. Wright spoke with him and convinced him to attend services that evening. The old warrior sat in the front row without moving, his hands clasped in his lap. Near the end of the service, he leapt to his feet, acknowledging that "the Jesus road was best," and, "Now we begin to think that the Christian white people love us."

Having converted the old reprobate, the church now hung back, reluctant to take him to their bosom. They detected, "a vein of self-importance in his talk." During the year that followed, Geronimo's religious mood swung from humility to arrogance, interspersed with drunken orgies, vindicating the church's decision not to grant him membership.

The church held the 1903 camp meeting in an oak grove on Medicine Bluff Creek. Geronimo was absent as services began; he had been seriously injured when Zi-yeh's pony threw him. But as the afternoon came on with its heat, Geronimo appeared, barely able to stay in the saddle. With Naiche beside him, Geronimo spoke through an interpreter: "He says that he is in the dark. He knows that he is not on the right road and he wants to find Jesus." The missionaries noted that "Naiche's fine, strong face blazed with joy."

The missionaries, Naiche, and other converts spent time with Geronimo, explaining the Christian religion. As the week of services ended, he confessed,

> I am old and broken by this fall I have had. I am without friends for my people have turned from me. I am full of sins, and I walk alone in the dark. I see that you missionaries have got a way to get sin out of the heart, and I want to take that better road and hold it till I die.

**APACHES GATHER AT 1903 DUTCH REFORMED
CHURCH CAMP MEETING AT FORT SILL.**

Still suspicious of his motives, the missionaries questioned him closely and found he truly wanted to become a Christian. They baptized him a week later. As he stepped from the water, the missionaries noted, "his face softened and became bright with joy."

Undoubtedly, Geronimo took his conversion seriously; religion had always been an important part of his life. But he found it difficult to reconcile his new Christian beliefs with those of Ussen. A few years later, he expressed some of his conflict to S.M. Barrett, who recorded his autobiography:

We [Apaches] believed that there is a life after this one, but no one ever told me what part of man lived after death. I have seen many men die; I have seen many human bodies decayed, but I have never seen that part that is called the spirit; I do not know what it is; nor have I yet been able to understand that part of the Christian religion.

Rather than discarding his old religion, Geronimo simply integrated the two, using from each what felt best to him. He continued with the familiar Apache ceremonies. He conducted a womanhood ceremony for his daughter Eva and continued his healing ceremonies out of sight of the Fort Sill authorities and the missionaries. When he said, in debating Christianity, "In many respects I believe Christianity to be better than the religion of my fathers. However, I believe that the Almighty has always protected me," he undoubtedly spoke of his Power that had promised him years before that he would not die at the hand of an enemy.

The loss of his human pleasures began to weigh on him. He had always loved to gamble, wager on horse races, and drink. Slowly, his old habits reasserted themselves. In 1907, the Rev. Leonard L. Legters, now the church pastor, had a stern meeting with him. When Geronimo complained that the rules of Christianity were "too strict" and reverted to the Apache religion, the church struck him from their roles.

For a time he seemed content with this, but his conflict with religion continued to burn deep beneath the surface. It erupted whenever death claimed his close friends — most often from old age — or family members. Since his captivity, his cherished son Chappo had died, he had lost two wives, along with children and grandchildren. His grandson Thomas Dahkeya, whom he cared for deeply, had died at 18. His daughter Eva was also sickly.

When other Apaches accused him of using his medicine-man powers to divert death to his family so he could live on as promised by his Power, Geronimo turned again to Christianity. He attended the 1908 camp meeting, professing his desire to become a Christian. But he still drank and gambled.

As he lay on his deathbed in the winter of 1909, this conflict continued to rage. In his delirium, he thought he saw his dead grandson Thomas, and Nat Kayitah, the son of one of the scouts who had tracked him into the Sierra Madre before his final surrender, who had died of pneumonia only a few days before. They urged him to become a Christian. He replied that he'd never been able to "follow the path" during his lifetime, although he had tried, and now it was too late. Why had they

waited so long? he asked. Because, they answered, he had refused to listen to the missionaries.

A curious story appears in *Among the Mescalero Apaches* by
Dorothy Emerson. In it, she cites a story told by Father
Albert Braun, who served at Mescalero for more than 30 years.
It concerned Father Isador Ricklin, a priest at Fort Sill during
the Apaches' incarceration there. "He had heard that his old
friend was failing, so he went to visit him," Braun said. "In
Geronimo's own language Father Ricklin asked, 'Have all the
horses been branded?' Geronimo told him they had. Father
Ricklin then asked Geronimo if he wanted to be branded a child
of Jesus. Geronimo said that he did, and Father Ricklin baptized him then."

If true, this is the only indication that Geronimo ever
came close to the Catholic religion (although his wife Zi-yeh
and infant daughter Lenna were baptized into Catholicism at
Mount Vernon, Alabama). It appears rather that in death he
reverted to the religion of his fathers.

Geronimo Rides the White Pony

Geronimo's nephew, Asa Daklugie, held the
old warrior's hand as he lay dying: "Old, feeble,
and dying, he had not lost his fighting spirit."

———◆———

I T WAS FEBRUARY 11, 1909, AND GERONIMO HAD A TERRIBLE thirst. He asked Eugene Chihuahua, son of his old warpath buddy Chihuahua, to buy him a bottle of whiskey. It was illegal for whites to sell liquor to the Apaches, but Chihuahua knew how to get around that. He asked a soldier he knew to buy the bottle, then waited in the bluster of a Oklahoma winter's day for the soldier's return. Handing the bottle to Geronimo, Chihuahua watched him ride away, bundled against the cold.

Geronimo had come into Lawton to sell some bows and arrows. Darkness had settled as he started home, but he wasn't concerned. The old warrior and his horse had ridden this trail often. Riding along a creek, he grew sleepy. In a stupor, he slid from his horse. It took too much effort to get up, so he closed his eyes and went to sleep.

The next morning, Mrs. Benedict Jozhe, wife of an Apache scout, saw his horse standing by the creek. She found Geronimo lying half in the water. Friends carried him home, but he'd caught cold. After three days, his condition worsened. Benedict Jozhe alerted the post surgeon.

When an ambulance pulled up to Geronimo's door, a dozen women, including Geronimo's wife Azul, surrounded him and refused to let the medical personnel take him to the small hospital that the Apaches called the "death house."

LEFT TO RIGHT: CHIHUAHUA, NAICHE, LOCO, NANA, AND GERONIMO IN ALABAMA, CIRCA 1890.

The post surgeon reported Geronimo's condition to Lieutenant Purington, in charge of Fort Sill, who, on February 15, sent a scout along with the ambulance to bring Geronimo to the hospital. The post surgeon diagnosed him with pneumonia and did not expect him to live through the night.

Geronimo knew he was dying, but his will to live fought on. He asked that his children, Robert and Eva, be brought from the Chilocco Indian School in northern Oklahoma. Possibly because he hated Geronimo — he had once said that Geronimo deserved to be hung — Purington sent a letter rather than a wire. Because of this, Robert and Eva did not start for their father's deathbed for two days. Still Geronimo hung on, determined to see his children one last time.

A devastated Chihuahua, who years later told author Eve Ball, "I feel I am responsible for the death of Geronimo," sat by his bed during the day, and Geronimo's nephew, Asa Daklugie, stayed with him at night. Besides feeling guilty for giving Geronimo the whiskey, Chihuahua also wished Geronimo a more glorious death: "The brave old warrior was dying, like a woman, in a hospital."

Geronimo talked of many things during the long wait for Robert and Eva. He remembered most of all the tragedy of Alope's death and his hatred of the Mexicans for causing him to lose so much. Thoughts of old comrades also came to mind. Daklugie said of those last hours:

[H]e talked of those 17 men who had eluded 5,000 men of the army of the United States; and eluded not only them, but also 2,500 Mexican soldiers — 7,500 men, well-armed, well-trained, and well-equipped against 17 whom they regarded as naked savages. The odds were only 500 to one against Geronimo, but still they could not whip him nor could they capture him.

Repeatedly during my vigil he expressed his regret for having surrendered. He wished that like Victorio he might have died fighting his enemies. Time after time he spoke of the warriors who had been so faithful to him. He even mentioned those whose loyalty had waned. Old, feeble, and dying, he had not lost his fighting spirit.

He regretted killing babies; he'd always had a soft spot for children. "In my hatred I would even take the little ones out of their cradles and toss them in the air," he'd said sometime before. "They would like this and would gurgle with glee, but when they came down I would catch them on my sharp hunting knife and kill them. I wake up groaning and very sad at night when I remember the helpless little children."

A member of his band, Charlie Smith, agreed. "It was terrible to see little children killed," he told Eve Ball. "There were times when I hated Geronimo for that."

Eva, too, filled Geronimo's thoughts. He asked Daklugie to take her in and look after her. Daklugie agreed. Because she was slight, Geronimo feared she would die in childbirth, and he asked Daklugie to see that she never married.

The white man's religion continued to plague Geronimo, even as he lay struggling for breath. His grandson, Thomas Dahkeya, and a friend, both of whom had died not long before, came to him in a vision and berated him for refusing to listen to the missionaries.

Still he clung to life throughout the second day. "As I sat

beside my uncle, I thought that he would never speak to me again and that the Apaches were losing the best they had," said Daklugie. "Now that we needed him most he was slipping away from us. Soon he would ride the ghost pony to the Happy Place."

By evening, even his indomitable spirit could hold on no longer. "Neither White Eye nor Indian medicine did any good. It was Geronimo's time to go," Chihuahua said.

He sank into a coma and died the following morning, February 17, at 6:15. "He died with his hand in mine," Daklugie said. "Geronimo's death hurt me as had those of my mother, father, and brothers."

Azul, his widow, prepared to kill his favorite pony as was custom, but other Apaches stopped her. Throughout the day, the old women of the tribe performed the proper grieving, groaning, wailing, and praying, as they filed through the little stone house where his body lay. The men stood silent and watchful.

The military gave the men a half-day off so they could attend the funeral set for 3 P.M. the next day. But it was delayed as the grief-stricken Robert and Eva had not yet arrived. When the train brought them a little after 3 P.M., the funeral procession, with Geronimo's body in an elaborately decorated hearse, started for the cemetery. They had dug his grave next to his wife Zi-yeh's, and around him lay the graves of many of his family members and comrades-in-arms.

Almost every member of the Apache tribe attended the funeral, as did many of Lawton's white population. Naiche spoke first of Geronimo's bravery and loyalty and how he had always stayed true to the peace treaty he had made with General Miles all those years before. He called Geronimo's refusal of Christianity his biggest failure and urged others to take a lesson from Geronimo's life.

Chihuahua interpreted for the Rev. Leonard Legters, who conducted the service. Legters lauded the fallen leader as probably the greatest war leader the Apaches had ever known. The pleasures of the body had been Geronimo's downfall, he continued, and echoing Naiche, urged the congregation to learn from Geronimo's life.

A local paper wrote that an old Apache woman wailed, "Everybody hated you; white men hated you, Mexicans hated you, Apaches hated you; all of them hated you. You have been good to us. We love you, we hate to see you go."

On the flip side, Arizona cowboy artist and author Ross Santee later wrote, "His passing was not mourned in Arizona."

James Kaywaykla told Eve Ball that before Geronimo died, he had asked his friends and relatives to tie his horse to a tree near his grave and place his other possessions on its east side. In three days time, he'd said, he would return for them. Azul, however, decided to bury his possessions with him, according to Apache custom. At the end of the service, his relatives stepped forward and placed items, including his riding whip and blanket, in his grave.

Daklugie said:

> We could not burn his house; and, though he had not died in it, that should have been done out of respect. We could not bury his best warhorse with him, but I saw that he had it for the journey. We placed his most treasured possessions in his grave — and he had some very valuable jewelry and blankets. He walks through eternity garbed as a chief in his ceremonial robes and his medicine hat. He rides a fine horse. He has his best weapons.

The Field Artillery School at Fort Sill erected a rock monument topped with a stone eagle at the head of his grave.

Today, the graves surrounding his above Cache Creek are a roll call of Apache history: Loco, Nana, Chihuahua; the descendents of Mangas Coloradas, Cochise, Victorio, Naiche, and Juh; and the scouts who gave their all to the U.S. military only to be exiled with the very renegades they helped track down.

So it ended. Geronimo never returned to Arizona. He sleeps forever in "foreign" ground. But his name, be it for good or evil, will live on as long as history itself.

PHOTOGRAPH CREDITS:

ACKNOWLEDGMENTS
Page 4   University of Southern Alabama Archives #C-15,017.

TABLE OF CONTENTS
Page 7   *True West* Magazine, Cave Creek.

INTRODUCTION
Page 13   Arizona Historical Society/Tucson.
Page 15   Smithsonian Institute #T15792.

SECTION ONE
Page 17   U.S. Army Artillery and Missile Center Museum, Fort Sill, #54.2.78.

CHAPTER THREE
Page 28   Florida State Archives.
Page 30   Arizona State Library, Archives and Public Records (ASLAPR), History
            and Archives Division, Phoenix.
Page 32   National Archives, #NWDNS-165-AI-11A.

SECTION TWO
Page 35   ASLAPR, History and Archives Division, Phoenix.

CHAPTER SIX
Page 40   Arizona Historical Society/Tucson.
Page 42   University of Oklahoma, Western History Collections.
Page 44   ASLAPR, History and Archives Division, Phoenix, #97-7478.

CHAPTER SEVEN
Page 52   Sharlot Hall Museum, Prescott, #HP SHM IN-A-155P.

CHAPTER EIGHT
Page 55   ASLAPR, History and Archives Division, Phoenix, #98-6066.
Page 64   ASLAPR, History and Archives Division, Phoenix.

CHAPTER TEN
Page 72   ASLAPR, History and Archives Division, Phoenix, #98-6108.

CHAPTER ELEVEN
Page 78   ASLAPR, History and Archives Division, Phoenix, #97-2621.
Page 80   Sharlot Hall Museum, Prescott, #HP SHM IN-A-160P.

CHAPTER TWELVE
Page 86   ASLAPR, History and Archives Division, Phoenix, #97-7936.

CHAPTER THIRTEEN
Page 93   Arizona Historical Society/Tucson.

CHAPTER FOURTEEN
Page 105   Arizona Historical Society/Tucson, #1153.
Page 107   ASLAPR, History and Archives Division, Phoenix.
Page 109   Arizona Historical Society/Tucson.

**GERONIMO WHILE IMPRISONED
IN ALABAMA, CIRCA 1890.**

WILD WEST COLLECTION

VOLUME 1

DAYS OF DESTINY

Fate Beckons Desperados & Lawmen

Every chain of events has a moment when fate intervenes and history changes. Here unfold true tales of desperados and lawmen facing days that marked their lives forever. 144 pages. Black and white illustrations and historical photographs. **#ADAP6 $7.95**

VOLUME 2

MANHUNTS & MASSACRES

Clever ambushes, horrific massacres, and dogged pursuits—each true story catapults the reader into savagery and suspense in Arizona Territory. 144 pages. Black and white historical photographs. **#AMMP7 $7.95**

VOLUME 3

THEY LEFT THEIR MARK

Heroes and Rogues of Arizona History

Indians, scouts, and adventurers of all sorts gallop through true stories of individualists who left their unique stamp—good or bad—on Arizona's early days. 144 pages. Black and white historical photographs. **#ATMP7 $7.95**

VOLUME 4

THE LAW OF THE GUN

Recounting the colorful lives of gunfighters, lawmen, and outlaws, Marshall Trimble explores the mystique of the Old West and how guns played into that fascination. 192 pages. Black and white historical photographs. **#AGNP7 $8.95**

VOLUME 5
TOMBSTONE CHRONICLES
Tough Folks, Wild Times

Silver transformed Tombstone into an oasis of decadence, culture, and reckless violence. Sample true stories from a town where anything could happen — and too often did. 144 pages. Black and white historical photographs. #AWTP8 $7.95

VOLUME 6
STALWART WOMEN
Frontier Stories of Indomitable Spirit

Tough enough to walk barefoot through miles of desert. Strong enough to fell a man with a blow. For danger and adventure, read riveting true portraits of gutsy women in the Old West. 144 pages. Black and white historical photographs. #AWWP8 $7.95

VOLUME 7
INTO THE UNKNOWN
Adventure on the Spanish Colonial Frontier

Centuries before Wyatt Earp and Billy the Kid, Spanish-speaking pioneers and gunslingers roamed into what now is the American West. They lived and died in a wild new world, driven by the power of the unknown. 144 pages. Illustrated. #ASCS9 $7.95

TO ORDER THESE BOOKS OR TO REQUEST A CATALOG, CONTACT:
Arizona Highways, 2039 West Lewis Avenue, Phoenix, AZ 85009-2893.
Or send a fax to 602-254-4505. Or call toll-free nationwide 1-800-543-5432.
(In the Phoenix area or outside the U.S., call 602-712-2000.)
Visit us at www.arizonahighways.com to order online.

ARIZONA HIGHWAYS
B O O K S

WILD WEST COLLECTION

VOLUME 8
RATTLESNAKE BLUES
Dispatches From A Snakebit Territory

Here are the stories you've never heard. Funny. Outrageous. Ridiculous. True accounts of the news, yarns, and utter lies about Arizona Territory that ran in newspapers of the day. 144 pages. Black and white historical photographs. **#ATHP0 $7.95**

VOLUME 9
BUCKSKINS, BEDBUGS & BACON

A vibrant collection of people settled the Southwest. They left stories of enduring a harsh land, putting up with isolation, and finding thrills in ways you would not imagine. 144 pages. Black and white historical photographs. **#ALFP0 $7.95**

VOLUME 10
DOUBLE CROSS
Treachery in the Apache Wars

Betrayal, outrage, and revenge tint the land with blood in true tales of the culture clash between settlers and the fiercely independent Apaches whose land they claimed. 144 pages. Black and white historical photographs. **#ABTP2 $7.95**

TO ORDER THESE BOOKS OR TO REQUEST A CATALOG, CONTACT:
Arizona Highways, 2039 West Lewis Avenue, Phoenix, AZ 85009-2893.
Or send a fax to 602-254-4505. Or call toll-free nationwide 1-800-543-5432.
(In the Phoenix area or outside the U.S., call 602-712-2000.)
Visit us at www.arizonahighways.com to order online.

ARIZONA HIGHWAYS
BOOKS